For Jane

Paul Turner

Let Us Pray

A Guide to
the Rubrics of Sunday Mass

A PUEBLO BOOK

Liturgical Press   Collegeville, Minnesota

A Pueblo Book published by Liturgical Press

Cover layout by David Manahan, o.s.b.
Cover illustration by Frank Kacmarcik, obl.s.b.

1 0   0 9   0 8   0 7   0 6   2   3   4   5

Library of Congress Cataloging-in-Publication Data

Turner, Paul, 1953–
    Let us pray : a guide to the rubrics of Sunday Mass / Paul Turner.
        p.   cm.
    "A Pueblo book."
    ISBN-13: 978-0-8146-6213-7 (pbk. : alk. paper)
    ISBN-10: 0-8146-6213-7 (pbk. : alk. paper)
    1. Mass—Handbooks, manuals, etc.   2. Catholic Church—Liturgy—Handbooks, manuals, etc.   I. Title.

BX2230.3.T87   2006
264'.02036—dc22

                                                    2005030658

Dedication

Contents

Acknowledgments

I wish to thank

    Gabe Huck, who planted

    litnetwk@listserv.nd.edu, which posted

    Paul Ford, who juxtaposed

    Sandra Dooley, Steve Janco, and James Field, who watered

    Ken Martin, who furrowed

    John Thomas, who farmed

    Mark Twomey, who harvested

    Jesus, who gave thanks

P. T.

Abbreviations

BB   Book of Blessings (Vatican City, 1984; U.S., 1989)

BLS   Built of Living Stones: Art, Architecture and Worship (Washington, D.C., 2000)

CB   Ceremonial of Bishops (Vatican City, 1984; U.S., 1989)

CDWDS   Congregation for Divine Worship and the Discipline of the Sacraments

DMC   Directory for Masses with Children (Vatican City, 1973; U.S., 1974)

GIRM   The General Instruction of the Roman Missal (Vatican City, 2002; U.S., 2003)

IOM   Introduction to the Order of Mass: A Pastoral Resource of the Bishops' Committee on the Liturgy (Washington, D.C., 2003)

LG   *Lumen Gentium* (Vatican II, Dogmatic Constitution on the Church)

LM   Introduction to the Lectionary for Mass (Vatican City, 1981; U.S., 1998)

LMC   Introduction, Lectionary for Masses with Children (U.S., 1993)

NDR   Norms for the Distribution and Reception of Holy Communion under Both Kinds in the Dioceses of the United States of America (Washington, D.C., 2002)

OM   The Order of Mass *(Ordo Missae)* (Vatican City, 2002)

PCS   Pastoral Care of the Sick: Rites of Anointing and Viaticum (Vatican City, 1972; U.S., 1983)

RCIA   Rite of Christian Initiation of Adults (Vatican City, 1972; U.S., 1988)

RM   Roman Missal *(Missale Romanum)* (Vatican City, 2002)

RS   *Redemptionis Sacramentum:* Instruction on the Eucharist (Vatican City, 2004; U.S., 2004)

SC   *Sacrosanctum Concilium* (Vatican II, The Constitution on the Sacred Liturgy)

USCCB   United States Conference of Catholic Bishops

Introduction

1.   Sunday Mass is the greatest miracle in the world: the celebration of the Eucharist. God speaks through the Scriptures. The Church offers a sacrifice of thanksgiving. The Holy Spirit transforms the gifts of bread and wine into the Body and Blood of Christ. The faithful share Communion with one another and with God. So nourished, the people of God go forth into the world to preach the gospel and to live by its demands.

2.   Sunday Mass follows what the liturgical documents have designed. The Catholic Church issues universal and regional norms for the celebration of Mass in the Roman Rite. The primary document is the General Instruction of the Roman Missal (GIRM). The Roman Missal (RM) is the book of prayers used by the priest at Mass. The introduction to the book is its General Instruction. The heart of the Missal is the Order of Mass (OM), a kind of script for the most common spoken or sung words and for the rubrics. Traditionally printed in red, the rubrics are instructions governing the actions of various participants—the priest and other ministers, as well as the assembly of the faithful. The rubrics ensure that what happens at Mass is what the Church intends.

3.   However, Sunday Mass is unpredictable. The rubrics do not explain everything that goes on. Accidents happen. Universal and local customs emerge. Almost every participant at every Mass fails to fulfill all that is expected and brings to the Mass more than is required. Yet the result is the same: the greatest miracle in the world, the celebration of the Eucharist.

4.   This book serves as a guide through the Mass. It presents the central details about the people who celebrate the Eucharist and about the setting where it takes place. It then follows the sequence of events in the Order of Mass. The reader will find the references to pertinent liturgical documentation, as well as commentary by the author. Cross-references to other paragraphs of this book are noted in the margin. The concluding sections consider a number of specific and general matters concerning the liturgical renewal.

5.   This book aims to describe a typical Sunday Mass at a parish church. It includes the role of deacons, because they serve in many parishes, though not in all. It refers to Masses with children to show how those celebrations may differ. The book does not consider in detail the Masses when the bishop presides, Masses with instituted acolytes and lectors, Masses at which only one minister participates, or concelebrated Masses. All these may take place in a parish, but more typical is a priest presiding over the gathered assembly, assisted by lay ministers. Almost every parish has some idiosyncrasies in its celebration of the Mass. This book does not attempt to cover them all.

6.   This book, then, is a guide to what happens—not just what should happen, but what does happen—at Sunday Mass. Some things happen in spite of the rubrics. Some things happen because of them. What happens inside the church is important, but so is what happens inside the heart. When the priest says, "Let us pray," his timing, pace, enunciation, gesture, and eye contact are all of great consequence. But so is something underneath it all: the prayer that happens as a result of this exhortation.

MAKING JUDGMENTS

7.   Various Church documents develop the comprehensive rubrics of Sunday Mass, making many pastoral judgments unnecessary. But the various participants at Mass make a number of judgments based on local variations, liturgical theology, historical precedent, scriptural influence, cultural sensitivity, or common sense.

THE DOCUMENTS

8.   The Catholic Church has issued an extensive body of documents to direct the celebration of the Mass. The principal documents are the 2002 RM with its GIRM and OM, published under the auspices of the Roman Congregation for Divine Worship and the Discipline of the Sacraments (CDWDS). Several other publications have been issued for the universal Church. The introduction to the Lectionary for Mass (LM) covers the Scripture readings for the Liturgy of the Word. The Directory for Masses with Children (DMC) explores celebrations with preadolescents. The Ceremonial of Bishops (CB), which contains directions for Masses at which a bishop presides, carries information pertinent to other celebra-

tions. The instruction *Redemptionis Sacramentum* (RS) from the CDWDS clarifies a number of restrictions in the celebration of Mass.

9. Other documents affect the Church in the United States. The Lectionary for Masses with Children (LMC), approved by the CDWDS, applied some principles of the universal DMC. The National Conference of Catholic Bishops (NCCB) issued guidelines on art, architecture, and worship under the title *Built of Living Stones* (BLS) in 2000. The United States Conference of Catholic Bishops (USCCB), formerly the NCCB, developed Norms for the Distribution and Reception of Holy Communion under Both Kinds in the Dioceses of the United States of America (NDR), a document recognized by the CDWDS in 2002. The USCCB also issued its own Introduction to the Order of Mass: A Pastoral Resource of the Bishops' Committee on the Liturgy (IOM). Not a legislative document, it is a "useful pastoral instrument for liturgical formation of the People of God" (xiii–xiv).

10. All these documents and countless others establish the guidelines for the celebration of Mass. The extent of this legislation renders it difficult for those who celebrate liturgy to master and manage the information. Many people both within and outside the Catholic Church are astounded at the breadth and nuance of this documentation. Some people find the preponderance of such directives an obstacle to spirit-driven prayer. Others find it the sure foundation upon which their authentic prayer is based. Without a doubt, though, one cannot understand or embrace the piety of the Catholic Church without coming to grips with its liturgical legislation. At its best, Sunday Mass observes a careful series of rubrics into which all present immerse themselves in a spirit of prayer before the Almighty. The Mass should not become an empty observance of rubrics; rather, the rubrics serve the Mass when participants infuse them with intention, devotion, and meaning. The Mass is more than its rubrics. When something beyond the rubrics happens, it does not always impede the power of the Spirit, who perfects our human efforts to reach the divine.

11. The liturgical books do not and cannot foresee everything that happens at Mass. They began their evolution as guidebooks for bishops. Only gradually have they incorporated directions for priests who preside and the assembly of the people who participate. There are still a few gaps, and the GIRM itself envisions certain accommodations and adaptations (23–26, 395–398). Within these spaces each liturgy subtly breathes a life of its own character. Each celebration of the Mass is a fresh encounter with the unchanging presence of God.

LOCAL VARIATIONS

12.   A diocese may issue its own directives for certain aspects of the Mass. For example, a bishop may establish local rules for Communion under both kinds (GIRM 283) and the choice of some texts (374).

13.   The architecture of the church will cause some adjustments as well. For example, several rituals presume that the church has sufficient space outside for people to gather, for instance, the Rite of Acceptance into the Order of Catechumens (Rite of Christian Initiation of Adults [RCIA] 48), the processions that begin Palm Sunday and conclude Holy Thursday, and the blessing of the fire at the Easter Vigil. Not all churches have the property. Some parishes would like to have more Communion stations, but their churches have little room for them. The placement of the sanctuary, tabernacle, sacristy, and baptismal font all affect the flow of the liturgy.

LITURGICAL THEOLOGY

14.   Liturgical theology applies the principles of tradition, symbols, and local expression to communal prayer. It influences decisions affecting both ordinary and special occasions. Ordinary decisions range from the choice of vessels to the wording of commentaries. On special occasions the local community decides how to recognize individuals, families, or parochial groups within Mass.

15.   This happens especially in Masses for children. "The free use of introductory comments will lead children to a genuine liturgical participation, but these should be more than mere explanatory remarks" (DMC 23). "In addition to the visual elements that belong to the celebration and to the place of celebration, it is appropriate to introduce other elements that will permit children to perceive visually the wonderful works of God in creation and redemption and thus support their prayer. The liturgy should never appear as something dry and merely intellectual" (DMC 35).

16.   Liturgical theology especially demands the expressive use of signs. The GIRM recognizes the importance of signs. For example,

> a.   The "actions and signs" of the Mass derive their meaning from texts based on Scripture (391).

> b.   "[S]acred buildings and requisites for divine worship should, moreover, be truly worthy and beautiful and be signs and symbols of heavenly realities" (288).

c.   Vestments are "a sign of the office proper to each minister" (335).

d.   The Roman Missal "must be preserved in the future as an instrument and an outstanding sign of the integrity and unity of the Roman Rite" (399).

e.   The dialogues and acclamations of the Mass "are not simply outward signs of communal celebration but foster and bring about communion between priest and people" (34).

f.   "Singing is the sign of the heart's joy" (39).

g.   A common posture "is a sign of the unity of the members of the Christian community gathered for the Sacred Liturgy; it both expresses and fosters the intention and spiritual attitude of the participants" (42).

h.   A bow is made to show reverence and honor "to the persons themselves or to the signs that represent them" (275).

i.   If kissing the altar or the Book of the Gospels is not in harmony with traditions or the culture of some region, bishops may establish "some other sign" in its place (273).

j.   When the gospel is proclaimed, "those present turn towards the ambo as a sign of special reverence to the Gospel of Christ" (133).

k.   The sacrifice of the cross "is made present under sacramental signs" (296).

l.   Peace is exchanged by means of a sign (82).

m.   Those receiving Communion first make a sign of reverence (160).

17.   Furthermore, the GIRM praises the expressive use of signs. It says the liturgy "is carried out through perceptible signs that nourish, strengthen, and express faith," and that when these are arranged in view of the circumstances of the people and the place, they "will more effectively foster active and full participation and more properly respond to the spiritual needs of the faithful" (20). For example, the Book of the Gospels and the Lectionary should serve "as signs and symbols of heavenly realities" and be "truly worthy, dignified, and beautiful" (349). Several judgments concerning the Communion rite are to be made on the basis of its sign:

a. The breaking of the bread "will bring out more clearly the force and importance of the sign of unity of all in the one bread, and of the sign of charity by the fact that the one bread is distributed among the brothers and sisters" (321).

b. The faithful are encouraged to receive Communion from hosts consecrated at the same Mass and to partake of the chalice when permitted, "so that even by means of the signs Communion will stand out more clearly as a participation in the sacrifice actually being celebrated" (85).

c. Communion under both kinds is encouraged "because this clearer form of the sacramental sign offers a particular understanding of the mystery in which the faithful take part" (14).

d. "Holy Communion has a fuller form as a sign when it is distributed under both kinds. For in this form the sign of the Eucharistic banquet is more clearly evident and clear expression is given to the divine will by which the new and eternal Covenant is ratified in the Blood of the Lord, as also the relationship between the Eucharistic banquet and the eschatological banquet in the Father's Kingdom" (281).

e. "The meaning of the sign demands that the material for the Eucharistic celebration truly have the appearance of food" (321).

f. "It is more in keeping with the meaning of the sign that the tabernacle in which the Most Holy Eucharist is reserved not be on an altar on which Mass is celebrated" (315).

g. The faithful "should be encouraged to seek to participate more eagerly in this sacred rite, by which the sign of the Eucharistic banquet is made more fully evident" (282).

Challenges such as these have fostered the application of the principle of liturgical signs to other aspects of the liturgy from the quantity of water in a sprinkling rite to the density of smoke in the thurible. When signs are large enough to be seen, loud enough to be heard, present enough to be touched, aromatic enough to be smelled, and delightful enough to be tasted, they reveal their deeper layers of meaning and enhance the prayers of the gathered faithful.

22

HISTORICAL PRECEDENT

18.   Some judgments for Sunday Mass are based on historical precedent. For example, the GIRM gives extensive directions for bishops, priests, deacons, acolytes, and lectors, but there is no clear list of responsibilities for an altar server. Nearly every parish church uses altar servers, but their duties vary slightly from one sanctuary to the next, based on local needs. The role of altar servers enjoys historical precedent, and local customs regarding their age and preparation govern their routine.

19.   Some priests retain habits no longer required of them since the reforms of Vatican II. They extend their arms for prayer no wider than the shoulders, they keep their fingers together after touching the consecrated host, or they reintroduce signs of the cross that have been omitted. Some priests do this out of personal piety, even though some of the faithful find these anachronisms distracting.

20.   At other parts of the Mass, people perform actions that have become local or regional customs. Some conclude the sign of the cross by kissing their thumb. Some strike their breast during the elevations. Many use holy water on exiting the church. None of these actions appear in the liturgical documents, but they are customs handed down. Such customs continue to be formed in individual churches and regions.

SCRIPTURAL INFLUENCE

21.   Sometimes a passage of the Bible influences liturgical judgments. Some people have sat in the back of the church because they identify with the tax collector in Jesus' parable, who entered the temple to pray but stood far off (Luke 18:13), even though the occasion was not communal prayer, much less Mass. The GIRM asks that substantial adaptations be submitted by bishops' conferences to the Apostolic See (395), but some parishes have overlooked the finer details of rubrics on the grounds that they promote the hypocritical pharisaism that Jesus condemned (e.g., Matthew 23). In some communities the texts and gestures have been altered to make them more inclusive, expressive, or comprehensible. Some people have rationalized these choices by their desire to continue the ministry of Jesus, who came to let the oppressed go free (Luke 4:18) and to preach love of neighbor as one of the great commandments (Matthew 22:39). "External action must be illuminated by faith and charity, which unite us with Christ and with one another and engender love for the poor and the abandoned" (RS 5).

22.   Jesus attracted the interest of disciples through the dramatic use of ordinary elements: the feeding of thousands with bread and fish (John 6:11); the changing of over a hundred gallons of water into wine (John 2:6, 9); the raising of Lazarus from the dead (John 11:44); the haul of 153 large fish (John 21:11); and his own baptism in a river of water (Mark 3:13). His exploitation of large symbols influences liturgical practice. Worshipers strive to have the same mind that was in Christ Jesus (Philippians 2:5).

Cultural Sensitivity

23.   Some judgments are influenced by the culture. Music, ritual, and the appearance of the environment for worship exhibit regional and ethnic variations.

24.   Many of the faithful debate the proper dress for worship. Some come formally; others do not. Some wear T-shirts bearing messages that others find offensive. Some dress too provocatively for the tastes of others. Some churches, such as St. Peter's Basilica in Vatican City, have strict requirements for the dress worn even by visitors. Others welcome all worshipers, no matter how they dress.

25.   Some feel as though the vessels, cloths, bread, and wine should resemble those used for meals at home, in order to show how marvelously God enters the most ordinary of human substances. Others feel as though these items should be more distinct from what people commonly experience, in order to show their otherworldly nature (cf. RS 117).

26.   At children's Masses some changes meet the needs of the assembly. "To encourage participation, it will sometimes be helpful to have several additions, for example, the insertion of motives for giving thanks before the priest begins the dialogue of the preface. In all this, it should be kept in mind that external activities will be fruitless and even harmful if they do not serve the internal participation of the children" (DMC 22).

Courtesy and Common Sense

27.   Some judgments about the liturgy are made from courtesy and common sense. For example, the people's response to the prayer of the faithful is variable. But if their response is to be something other than one they customarily say, someone will need to announce it, even though there is no such liturgical text. If the wind blows a candle out, a server relights it, even though there is no rubric for lighting candles during the liturgy.

28.   Because so much ritual takes place at Mass, even things that are not ritual by nature begin to appear that way. If Communion ministers visibly wash their hands before approaching the altar, the action intended as a courtesy will appear as part of the ritual.

VARIETY AND CONSTANCY IN THE MASS

29.   Sunday Mass derives its spirituality from constancy as well as variety. The principal structures remain the same, and they deepen the spiritual life through repetition. But other elements shift slightly, enabling worshipers to enjoy the complex mystery of God from various views.

30.   Some people struggle with constancy, others with variety. Adolescents, for example, often complain that Sunday Mass is boring. The very repetitions that appeal to regular churchgoers make prayer difficult for those experiencing more variety in life. Similarly, the changes intended to add life to a particular celebration make it difficult for those who prefer to pray predictably. The American culture is rich in entertainment opportunities and poor in its ability to meditate. It contributes to the liturgy ideas for better communication at public gatherings, but it interferes with people's ability to focus on God in prayer.

31.   Unusual things happen at any given Mass. Some are planned, some are accidental. Some make the Mass more prayerful, some make it more obtuse. All the faithful are called to worship at Mass as best they can. Sometimes their disappointment with the proceedings becomes uncharitable, impairing their own responsible participation. Worship is handicapped when some people presume the worst of those planning and executing the liturgy, labeling as "abuses" honest attempts at deepening the contemporary community's experience of the divine or assuming "rigidity" in those who seek uniformity in prayer. At the Eucharist people gather to give thanks and praise to God, to listen to the Scriptures, and to share Communion with God and one another. If those present are truly participating, their complaints about nettlesome details will be washed away in the cleansing waters of charity.

32.   Sunday Mass should always follow the liturgical books. It should be deliberate, planned, and spiritual, but open to the unexpected, where God is also present. Regardless of human effort, Sunday Mass is always divine. The faithful are to enter the Mass with purity of heart and a spirit of charity. Then they will be prepared to meet God.

Introductory Rites

33.   The purpose of the introductory rites "is to ensure that the faithful who come together as one establish communion and dispose themselves to listen properly to God's word and to celebrate the Eucharist worthily" (GIRM 46).

BEFORE MASS

THE GATHERING OF THE PEOPLE

The Assembly

34.   First the people gather. The rubrics for Mass begin with a terse phrase in Latin: *Populo congregato* (OM 1; GIRM 47, 120). It means "After the people have gathered." That phrase replaces the first two words of the pre-Vatican II rubrics: *Sacerdos paratus,* meaning "After the priest is ready." The Missal of the Second Vatican Council widened the vision of the Mass from the very first words. As the Council's Dogmatic Constitution on the Church began its description of membership with the People of God (LG 9–17), so the liturgy begins its description of the Mass with the people assembled.

35.   At Mass "Christ is really present in the very liturgical assembly gathered in his name" (GIRM 27). He is present when the Church prays and sings (SC 7). Christ is present in the minister, the word, and substantially and continuously under the Eucharistic species, but Christ is also really present in the people.

36.   When most of those who gather are preadolescent children, certain adaptations may be made throughout the liturgy on their behalf (IOM 17). But even when they are not in the majority, "some account should be taken of their presence" (DMC 17). The local bishop has the authority to apply adaptations allowed for Masses with children in the majority to Masses with children in the minority (DMC 19). He may, for example, authorize a broader usage of the Eucharistic Prayers composed for children

at a celebration such as First Communion, even if preadolescent children are in the minority (Eucharistic Prayers for Masses with Children 14).   *534*

37.   The duty of the people is to "form a holy people . . . to give thanks to God and offer the spotless Victim not only through the hands of the priest but also together with him, so that they may learn to offer themselves" (GIRM 95). The people gather for a spiritual purpose. They should have a "deep religious sense" and "charity toward brothers and sisters who participate with them." Jesus said that the greatest commandment is love, so the people are commanded to love one another, to give thanks to God, and to give themselves in the offering of the Mass. It is not just the priest who offers the Mass. The people do not "attend" Mass. All who come offer together the sacrifice (cf. RS 38). "Thus the participation of the lay faithful too in the Eucharist . . . cannot be equated with mere presence, and still less with a passive one, but is rather to be regarded as a true exercise of faith and of the baptismal dignity" (RS 37).   *516*

38.   Even before coming to church, the people should prepare "by learning beforehand more about the Sacred Scripture" (LM 48). People will be more ready to participate if they have prayed over the readings for that Mass during the preceding week.   *298*

Arriving

39.   Outside many churches a bell is rung to call the faithful to Mass. Neither the GIRM nor the OM says that this should be done or when it may be done. However, "it is an ancient practice to summon the Christian people to the liturgical assembly or to alert them to important happenings in the local community by means of bells" (BLS 99). The Order for the Blessing of Bells says, "It is an ancient practice to summon the Christian people to the liturgical assembly" (BB 1305). "The peal of bells calls us to the celebration of the liturgy" (1312). The blessing itself includes this petition: "May your people hasten to your church when they hear the call of this bell" (1319). The alternate blessing asks that the voice of the bells "prompt us to come gladly to this church" (1320). Some churches have a bell suspended between the sanctuary and a sacristy adjacent to it. In those cases a server may ring it before the procession moves through that doorway. But this practice misses the point: A bell rung outside summons people inside. It would be sensible to ring the outside bell several times a few minutes before Mass begins. The practice summons worshipers and announces the sacredness of this time to non-believers as well.

40.   People should avoid arriving late. In the past, Catholics were taught that they could arrive as late as the offertory and still fulfill their obliga-

837 tion. The liturgical documents issued since the Second Vatican Council never make such an allowance. "The intimate connection between the Liturgy of the Word and the Liturgy of the Eucharist in the Mass should prompt the faithful to be present right from the beginning of the celebration" (LM 48).

41.   Upon arriving at church, people will naturally greet one another. Ushers or greeters may assist. Some greeters are distinct from ushers who take up the collection and direct processions (GIRM 105cd). Everyone is called

51, 54, 414 to extend hospitality, not just the ushers. Some churches have a narthex or gathering area large enough for people to visit before the service. Those arriving at church will recognize that they are "invited guests of the Lord himself . . . if they are made welcome by representatives of the community and acknowledged informally by their neighbors" (IOM 23).

42.   If there is a special collection of food or articles for the poor, people

417 may set them in a common area before reaching their seats.

43.   Upon entering the church, many people sign themselves with holy water. This practice is not mentioned in either the GIRM or the OM, but the CB says, "It is an old and honored practice for all who enter a church to dip their hand in a font (stoup) of holy water and sign themselves with

827 the sign of the cross as a reminder of their baptism" (110).

44.   Some churches empty the holy water stoups during Lent in correspondence with the desert symbolism that opens the season and in longing for the blessing of new baptismal water at Easter. However, the CDWDS declared the practice "not permitted" in a letter dated March 14, 2000, because Lent "is also a season rich in symbolism of water and baptism" and because sacramentals should be available to the faithful year round. "The practice of the church has been to empty the Holy Water fonts on the days of the Sacred Triduum in preparation of the blessing of the water at the Easter Vigil, and it corresponds to those days on which the Eucharist is not celebrated (i.e., Good Friday and Holy Saturday)" (Prot. N. 569/00/L).

45.   Some people perform devotional exercises upon entering the church. For example, they visit an area where religious images are located, make a contribution, and light a candle. Such candles symbolize the believer's desire to make his or her petition known to heaven. When such devo-

tional areas are located outside the nave, they encourage private prayer in private places and communal prayer in the nave.

121, 128, 129

SEATING

46.   Places for the assembly to sit are in the nave. The faithful should have a place that "facilitates their active participation" (GIRM 294). They should be able to participate "visually and spiritually" and to hear without difficulty (311). Most churches have pews or chairs with kneelers. A few have pews or chairs and no kneelers. Whatever the furniture arrangement, people should be able to assume the postures of the liturgy and enter the Communion procession (311).

47.   Extraordinary ministers of Communion will normally take their place with the assembly in the nave. They need not have special seating in the sanctuary nor join the entrance procession (IOM 21). 161

48.   Some parishes supply assisted-hearing devices, large-print materials, and American sign language translation for members who need such aid. Some churches reserve special spaces for persons who use wheelchairs. Some houses of worship may be exempt from civil legislation requiring wheelchair accessibility from the street to the nave and to restrooms, but the spirit of the Eucharist will motivate congregations to make their space accessible especially to those suffering from infirmities. 63

49.   Many churches have a cry room for wailing infants and those who care for them. Usually this is a room adjacent to the nave from which people watch Mass through a glass partition. Some people use cry rooms by preference or because of lack of other seating. Cry rooms generally do not facilitate active participation. They do not adhere to one of the principles for the form and arrangement of the nave: "the community worships as a single body" (BLS 52). The liturgical documents never recommend a cry room for "infants who as yet are unable or unwilling to take part in the Mass," but the DMC envisions that "parish helpers [take] care of them in a separate area" (16), so that the parents can focus on worship. 800

50.   In Masses with children in which only a few adults participate, the children should sit in a space "suited to the number of participants . . . where the children can act with a feeling of ease according to the requirements of a living liturgy that is suited to their age." Such a space may even be outdoors (DMC 25). The local bishop may authorize these accommodations also for Masses with only a few children (DMC 19).

51.   Ushers or greeters help people find a place (IOM 23). The GIRM describes "those who, in some places, meet the faithful at the church entrance, lead them to appropriate places, and direct processions" (105d). The IOM says ushers welcome people "at the door, providing them with all necessary books and aids, and helping them find their places" (23). In the past, ushers stereotypically performed this role in a perfunctory manner. Many churches now encourage them to seat people with a more sincere welcome. Some greeters hand out the weekly parish news bulletin before Mass, but non-liturgical materials distract people from prayer during the Mass. It is better to make the bulletin available after the service: As people are dismissed, they immediately see ways to serve God throughout the coming week. Ushers or greeters may ask latecomers to remain standing near the door of the church until after the collect (opening prayer) or during the gospel acclamation. Latecomers are less conspicuously seated while the whole assembly is changing its posture.

Sitting

52.   Before taking their place, the faithful make a sign of reverence. Most Catholics genuflect. A genuflection is made by lowering one's right knee to the ground to signify adoration (GIRM 274; CB 69). If lowering the left knee is easier, common sense would permit it. Some people place one hand on the pew for support. Many make the sign of the cross while genuflecting. Some lower the knee only part way to the ground. Although it is common for Catholics to genuflect before taking their place, it is appropriate only if the tabernacle is present in the sanctuary (GIRM 274). In churches where the tabernacle is in a side chapel, the faithful should "adore the blessed sacrament, either by visiting the blessed sacrament chapel or at least by genuflecting" (CB 71). Such a genuflection could be made from one's seat in the direction of the tabernacle. But another reverence is more appropriate in churches where the tabernacle is not in the sanctuary: The faithful should make a profound bow to the altar (GIRM 275b; CB 68). Catholics who find this odd may be surprised that the altar, not the tabernacle, is the center of attention for the Mass (GIRM 299).

53.   Participants may select a seat anywhere in the nave. In many parishes Catholics avoid the front seats, and the back rows often fill up first. It would be a far greater sign of participation if the eagerness of the Catholic faithful to celebrate the Eucharist moved them to occupy the front rows first.

54.   When first taking one's seat, it would be appropriate to greet those nearby. It would be courteous for churchgoers to make room for others arriving after them, to acknowledge their presence, offer them a hymnal or assist some other need. People coming to Mass will more readily appreciate that they are invited guests of the Lord himself "if they are made welcome by representatives of the community and acknowledged informally by their neighbors" (IOM 23).   41

55.   The liturgical documents give no further instructions for what the faithful do once they have taken their place. Many people kneel and pray in silence. Some read materials they brought along or picked up on their way into church. This time of silent personal prayer is so important to worshipers that even some of those arriving late kneel for a moment before joining the community's prayer.

56.   The GIRM asks for silence in the church, sacristy, and adjacent areas before Mass (45). Silence will naturally be broken when people greet one another on their way into the church, when musicians play and choirs sing preludes to the service, or whenever the cantor asks the faithful to rehearse music (IOM 18). Some people like to recite the rosary together before Mass begins. In a few parishes the cantor breaks the silence by asking people to observe a few moments of silence before the Mass begins. Although the GIRM does not precisely envision any of these possibilities, they are practical ways that silence is broken before Mass. On the other hand, some people believe that all silent prayer should cease for the announcement of minor alarms, such as a car parked in the lot with its lights on; it would be better to make jumper cables available after Mass. All participants will help the management of silences and sounds if they switch off cell phones and pagers before entering the church.

Seating for Ministers

57.   Some other ministers take their places before Mass begins. The sacristan (GIRM 105a), who arranges what is necessary for Mass, may be seated when all is prepared. In the absence of the sacristan, the priest, servers, or a volunteer usually sets up.

58.   The choir and other musicians take places that facilitate their full participation (GIRM 103, 294, 312). The cantor or choir director will lead the people's singing (104) from an area apart from the ambo. The documents do not say where, but many parishes establish a music area. A

choir loft behind the congregation usually does not serve as well as an area visible and connected to the participants. "The ministers of music are most appropriately located in a place where they can be part of the assembly and have the ability to be heard" (BLS 90). Many parishes establish a cantor stand in the music area. Usually it is large enough to hold music, has appropriate lighting and microphone availability, and is located where people can see it, yet it does not compete with the ambo in size and placement. The texts at some Masses are completely spoken, and musicians are not used.

73, 144, 306

59.   A commentator may make brief explanations at the service, but this role is often eliminated. When speaking, the commentator stands in front, but not at the ambo (GIRM 105b). In some parishes the commentator uses the cantor stand.

58, 73

60.   The GIRM never recommends special seating for ushers or greeters, but in many parishes the ushers reserve the back pew or occupy a separate ushers' room. Seating ushers near the doors of the church advantageously places them where they can tend to the needs of all those arriving, even those coming in late. However, ushers at the back of church should be all the more careful to participate at the Mass, not simply to observe it, or worse to ignore the liturgy by spending too much time visiting in the narthex.

41, 51

FURNITURE

Sanctuary

61.   The principal furnishings of the sanctuary are the altar, the ambo, and the chair. Many sanctuaries include the tabernacle, but it is not essential to the liturgy as these other furnishings are. "The sanctuary is the place where the altar stands, where the Word of God is proclaimed, and where the priest, the deacon, and the other ministers exercise their offices" (GIRM 295).

62.   The materials for the furnishings should be noble, durable, and well suited for sacred use (GIRM 301, 326). Marble is traditional, but wood, other stone, and metal may be used in the United States.

63.   Many churches have made their sanctuaries accessible to persons with disabilities. "Methods of elevation can be found that still allow access to the altar by ministers who need wheelchairs or who have other disabilities" (BLS 59). Other sanctuaries are not accessible, even though

the NCCB stated in June 1995: "Parish sacramental celebrations should be accessible to persons with disabilities and open to their full, active and conscious participation, according to their capacity . . . . These adaptations are an ordinary part of the liturgical life of the parish" ("Guidelines for the Celebration of the Sacraments with Persons with Disabilities" 3). *48*

Altar

64.   The altar is also a table. It is the altar of the sacrifice of the cross and the table of thanksgiving for the Eucharist (GIRM 296). The altar is "the center toward which the attention of the whole congregation of the faithful naturally turns" (299).

65.   Ideally, there should be only one altar in a church (GIRM 303). Older churches were built with several altars to facilitate the celebration of more than one Mass at a time during the centuries when priests were not allowed to concelebrate. A single altar signifies "the one Christ and the one Eucharist of the Church." An old high altar of artistic merit may be retained, but a freestanding, fixed altar should be used for Mass.

66.   A church's altar should be fixed, not movable, because it signifies Christ Jesus, the living stone (1 Peter 2:4; cf. Ephesians 2:20); (GIRM 298).

67.   The altar should be apart from the wall. People will need to walk around it, and the priest should be able to celebrate Mass facing the people (GIRM 299). However, in some old sanctuaries one may find no other altar than the one against the wall. The OM contains a surprising number of expressions presuming that Mass facing the *wall* is normative. The manifold retention of such rubrics overlooks the clear preference of GIRM 299.

68.   Relics of saints may be embedded in or under the altar (GIRM 302). The practice is "fittingly retained" but is not obligatory. It recalls the habit of the early Church of celebrating the Eucharist at the tombs of martyrs. In parts of the world where martyrs are both gratefully and regretfully few, the authentic relics of other saints may be used. But no relics are required.

69.   The altar is covered with at least one white cloth (GIRM 117). More than one cloth may be used. Some churches adorn the altar with cloths denoting the color of the season or suggesting a spirit for the celebration (346). These are permitted as long as a white cloth lies over them, covering *90*

the top of the altar, not necessarily its sides (304). Linen is traditional, but no specific kind of material is required for the altar cloths.

70. In some churches the corporal has also been placed on the altar before Mass to simplify the preparation of the altar and the gifts. Few people would even notice it there. But the corporal will collect any particles or drops of the consecrated bread and wine, so it more properly *107, 419,* arrives for the Liturgy of the Eucharist and is removed afterwards.
718, 774

71. Before Mass, the altar should be clear. Apart from its cloth, nothing else is to be on the altar except possibly the candles, the cross, or the Book *117, 119* of the Gospels (GIRM 117, 306). In some parishes a stand for the Book of *177* the Gospels is set on the altar before Mass. A discreet microphone may also rest there. But at the start of Mass the altar should be clear of the *419* Missal, the chalice, and other items for the Liturgy of the Eucharist.

Ambo

72. The ambo is an elevated desk, pulpit, or lectern from which the readings are proclaimed. It should be stationary, not movable, in keeping with the dignity of God's word. It is best situated where the assembly can naturally turn their attention for the Liturgy of the Word (GIRM 260, 309).

73. The ambo is used for the readings, including the responsorial psalm, and for the *Exsultet* at the Easter Vigil. It may be used for the homily and *290, 361,* the prayer of the faithful. Only a minister of the word—a lector, psalmist, *391* deacon, or priest—speaks or sings from the ambo (GIRM 309). The com- *58, 59, 799* mentator and songleader conduct their ministries elsewhere (LM 33).

74. The design of the ambo should harmonize with that of the altar (LM 32). It may be decorated continuously or on solemn occasions (33). It should be large enough to accommodate several ministers at a time. *285* It should have adequate lighting for reading and be equipped with a microphone if necessary (34).

Chair

187 75. The chair is the place from which the priest presides over the assembly and directs its prayer (GIRM 310) at the beginning of the Mass. He remains at the chair through the readings, unless he proclaims the gospel from the ambo. The chair may also be used for the homily (136) and the conclusion of Mass. "Chair" designates the piece of furniture and the area immediately in front of it. When the priest makes the sign of the cross at the beginning of Mass, for example, he is at the chair but not in it.

361, 784

192

76.   Normally, the chair is "in a position facing the people at the head of the sanctuary." But where the distance between the apse and the nave is great, or where the tabernacle occupies the area behind the altar, or for other good reasons, the chair may be elsewhere (GIRM 310). In many churches the chair is located close to the front of the sanctuary to shorten the distance between priest and people.

198, 229, 239, 785

77.   Some churches set a lectern at the chair, on which the priest places notes, the Missal, a Lectionary, or his homily. But the documents never envision such a lectern, preferring the use of servers and the ambo for these functions.

252, 73

78.   The chair is located in the sanctuary to facilitate the priest's ministry and to designate his office within the whole people of God (GIRM 294). However, the chair should never resemble a throne (310). The seating in church respects the diversity of ministries, but it "should nevertheless bring about a close and coherent unity that is clearly expressive of the unity of the entire holy people" (294). Attention is thus drawn to the holiness of the mysteries, not the individuality of ministers.

79.   In many churches the chair is made from materials and a design that are in harmony with the altar and the ambo, the other main furnishings of the sanctuary. It may also be designed to agree with the seating of the assembly, showing the unity of the people of God.

74

OTHER FEATURES

Books

80.   The books used for the liturgy should be "worthy, dignified, and beautiful," because they serve as signs and symbols of heavenly realities (GIRM 349; LM 35). This is especially true of the Book of the Gospels and the Lectionary, which hold the word of God. But the elegant appearance of other books—for example, those containing the prayers of the priest and the songs of the community—would also dignify the celebration.

81.   When these books are not in use, they are usually stored in cabinets or on shelves in the sacristy. Some churches have created special shelving

for the Lectionaries and the Book of the Gospels to set them apart from all other books.

82.   Readers sometimes have proclaimed the word of God from materials of lesser quality, such as paperback worship aids or photocopies. This practice weakens the effect of the Liturgy of the Word. "Because of the dignity of the Word of God, the books of readings used in the celebration are not to be replaced by other pastoral aids, for example, by leaflets printed for the preparation of the readings by the faithful or for their personal meditation" (LM 37).

83.   Before Mass begins, the Lectionary should be placed on the ambo (GIRM 118b, 128). If it is also opened to the proper page, it will minimize
291   distractions when the lector approaches the ambo for the first reading. No ceremony accompanies this placement, but liturgical books are best handled with dignity.

84.   The Book of the Gospels may be carried in the entrance procession or placed on the altar before Mass begins (GIRM 117, 120d). A beautifully designed Book of the Gospels attracts greater respect than other books of readings. At first it was recommended for "cathedrals and at least the larger, more populous parishes and the churches with a larger attendance" (LM 36), but the GIRM's frequent reference to this book implies more widespread usage. One is commonly found in churches
176   of any size.

85.   The Missal should be placed next to the priest's chair (GIRM 118a). The 2002 English translation of the GIRM uses the word "Missal" for the book that has been called "Sacramentary" in the United States. In the Middle Ages Sacramentaries contained presidential prayers and Lectionaries contained readings; later these functions were combined into books called "Missals." The Second Vatican Council separated the Missal back into two books, putting all the readings in a Lectionary. The other book retained the title *Missale Romanum,* but the Vatican approved naming it "Sacramentary" in English. The GIRM now calls the book "Missal," even in English. "Missal" is a closer cognate to the Latin word and harmonizes the title with other vernacular languages.

86.   The Missal is produced with a number of tabs marking places of repeated use and ribbons to mark places of changeable use within the
199, 253,   book. Eucharistic Prayers, for example, are generally marked with tabs
542, 805   glued onto the page, but the presidential prayers for a given day are usu-

20

ally marked with movable ribbons. The ribbons for a particular Mass are 522 usually moved to the side of the book for easy reference. The purpose of the ribbons is defeated if they are not set in place before the Mass begins. A good presider will not flip pages during Mass to locate a place that should have been marked earlier. The ribbons often come in various colors. The colors have no significance apart from helping distinguish one marked place from another.

87.   A hymnal may also be placed next to the priest's chair (GIRM 118a). This instruction was probably included to encourage the priest to sing along with the assembly, but it neglects some practical matters. If there is an entrance procession, surely the priest should be singing from the hymnal as he enters. He cannot do this if the hymnal is next to his chair. In addition, a thorough treatment of liturgical books would also require the placement of hymnals near the seating for the assembly. But this is the only reference to a hymnal in the entire GIRM.

88.   Some ministers use a binder to gather other notes for the liturgy. For example, the freely composed texts for the introductions (GIRM 31) or the closing to the prayer of the faithful (71) could be kept in a binder for the priest or slipped into pockets at the front and back of the Missal. Another binder could contain the intentions for the general intercessions. 207, 220, 387, 393

Vesture

89.   Ministers vest for Mass (GIRM 120, 171). The vestments distinguish the offices of those who wear them. They also contribute to the beauty of the Mass (GIRM 335). Sacred vesture helps establish an environment conducive to ceremony, so central to Catholic piety.

90.   The priest wears an alb, a stole, and a chasuble (GIRM 337). If the alb does not cover his ordinary clothing at the neck, he dons an amice first. If the alb is too long, he wears a cincture to lift it from the waist (336). The stole drapes from behind the neck over both shoulders (340). The chasuble, the priest's signature vestment, cloaks the other ones (337). The stole and chasuble take the color of the liturgical day: green for Ordinary Time; violet for Advent and Lent; red for the celebration of the Passion, Pentecost, and martyrs; and white or other festive colors for Christmas, Easter, and other solemn days. Rose may be worn on the Third Sunday of Advent and the Fourth Sunday of Lent (346). 92, 124

91.   The chasuble is worn "over the alb and stole" (GIRM 337). Some priests wear the stole over the chasuble. Some vestments have been made

for this purpose, accentuating the design or body of the stole and distinguishing it from the one worn by deacons. Some priests have gone a step further, illogically wearing over the chasuble a stole designed to be worn under it. The tradition is that the stole is worn underneath, and the chasuble is the more visible sign of the priest's liturgical ministry. Vesture is to distinguish the liturgical offices without distracting attention from the Eucharist.

92. The deacon wears an alb, a stole, and a dalmatic (GIRM 171, 338; cf. LM 54). His stole is worn over the left shoulder and crossed at the right hip (340). The dalmatic may be reserved for solemn celebrations. The CDWDS recommends wearing the dalmatic regularly (RS 125). However, many deacons exercise the option to avoid it because it obscures the design of their stole, which at once identifies their office and distinguishes them from priests more visibly than the dalmatic does. Some deacons wear the stole over the dalmatic, but the tradition is to wear it underneath. The stole and dalmatic take the color of the liturgical day (GIRM 346). If necessary, the deacon also wears an amice and cincture (336).

91
90

93. The lector wears "approved attire" (GIRM 194). The expression is ambiguous because some lectors are instituted and others are not. A man preparing for ordination to the diaconate or priesthood will be instituted as a lector by a bishop in a formal ceremony. An instituted lector wears an alb, as well as an amice and a cincture if needed (336), and holds among his responsibilities the reading of the word of God at Mass. However, other lay people, both men and women, may proclaim the readings and commonly do. Rarely in Catholic parishes is the lector an instituted male. In the United States non-instituted lectors "may wear the alb or other suitable vesture or other appropriate and dignified clothing" (GIRM 339, IOM 57). Most parishes ask lectors to dress in a way that would not distract people's attention from the reading (cf. LM 54).

163, 189,
282

288

94. Acolyte is another instituted ministry given to men in preparation for diaconate and priesthood. Few parishes have instituted acolytes. Most divide the acolyte's responsibilities among extraordinary ministers of Holy Communion and altar servers. An instituted acolyte wears an alb with optional amice and cincture (GIRM 336), but other lay ministers in the United States "may wear the alb or other suitable vesture or other appropriate and dignified clothing" (339). In most parishes altar servers wear either an alb with optional cincture or a cassock and surplice.

155

Eucharistic ministers commonly exercise their ministry in the clothes they wear to church.

709

95.   In some parishes lay ministers wear an ornamental pin, badge, or cross identifying their role, but the liturgical documents neither promote nor discourage this.

96.   The GIRM makes no mention about the clothes of the assembly. Some people like to dress up for Mass and are disappointed by those who dress casually. Others find casual clothing more conducive to prayer. The description of clothing for lay ministers in the United States could apply to the assembly as well: "appropriate and dignified" (339).

Vessels

97.   The vessels for Mass resemble those used in homes for meals, but they should be "clearly distinguishable from those intended for everyday use" (GIRM 332).

98.   Vessels that hold the Body and Blood of the Lord are traditionally made from precious metal (GIRM 328), but in the United States other materials may be used as long as they "are suited to sacred use and do not easily break or deteriorate" (329). The CDWDS classifies glass, earthenware, and clay as materials "that break easily" (RS 117). However, not all such substances are so easily breakable, and many such vessels have been consecrated and put into use for generations, often fashioned in faith by local artisans. Some bishops have permitted the use of these vessels for the Eucharist. The inside bowls of chalices and other vessels that hold the consecrated wine should be non-absorbent (GIRM 330).

99.   A chalice is the cup from which the Blood of Christ is consumed at Communion. Usually it is a bowl resting on a stem, with or without a node. The design and number of chalices changed when the Second Vatican Council authorized Communion under both forms for the assembly. Formerly a chalice was just large enough for the priest alone to sip its contents. Now "a chalice of sufficiently large size or several chalices are prepared" (GIRM 285) when all are invited to partake of it. The 468, 720 American bishops suggest that chalices "need to be large enough to be shared, easily handled between minister and communicant, and easily tilted by the communicant for drinking" (IOM 51). In many parishes the priest drinks from a chalice that resembles the ones used for everyone else to demonstrate the oneness of those who share Communion. The

CDWDS, however, prefers "a main chalice of larger dimensions, together with smaller chalices" (RS 105).

100. A paten is the plate that holds the bread for consecration. The design of the paten also changed in the twentieth century. For many hundreds of years, people did not receive Communion very often. When they did, they received from hosts previously consecrated and reserved in the tabernacle. The paten was just large enough to hold the host the priest would eat. Now "a large paten may appropriately be used; on it is placed the bread for the priest and the deacon as well as for the other ministers and for the faithful" (GIRM 331). "The fundamental Eucharistic symbolism of many sharing in the one bread and one cup is more clearly expressed when all the bread is contained in a single vessel and all the wine in one vessel" (IOM 51), but some parish Masses are attended by hundreds if not thousands of communicants, making it difficult to preserve this ideal.

101. Traditionally, the paten looks like a plate, but in many churches it resembles a broad bowl. A vessel with some depth is more able to contain the bread for the entire assembly and keep it from spilling.

102. A ciborium is a vessel for the distribution or reservation of consecrated bread. At first glance, many ciboria resemble chalices: a bowl raised above a stem. The primary difference is that ciboria have lids. Other ciboria are designed without stems and resemble lidded bowls. The American bishops caution that vessels used to distribute the Body of Christ should "have the form of patens and ciboria rather than of chalices" (IOM 51).

103. Flagons or pitchers may be prepared to hold the wine. This suggestion appeared in the 1985 NCCB document *This Holy and Living Sacrifice* (40), an early directive for Communion under both kinds. The GIRM does not refer to these vessels by name, nor does it explain how a quantity of wine is brought to the altar and poured into separate vessels. Originally NDR 37 said of the *Lamb of God*, "The deacon or priest . . . if necessary, pours the Precious Blood into enough additional chalices as are required for the distribution of Holy Communion." Even here the vessel holding the Precious Blood was not named. Logic and the earlier documentation called for some kind of flagon. However, RS 105 changed the legislation: "the pouring of the Blood of Christ after the consecration from one vessel to another is completely to be avoided." Flagons may be used to carry the wine to the altar for the preparation of the gifts and to pour it into chalices at that time, but not for the consecration or the pouring of the Precious Blood during the *Lamb of God*. In parishes with many commu-

nicants, this disturbs the balance between the preparation of the bread and the preparation of the cup and visibly detracts from the important sign of one bread and one cup. Some bishops have permitted the pouring of cups during the breaking of the bread. 468
648, 854

104. Cruets containing water and wine are to be set at the credence table before Mass (GIRM 118c). Many parishes have matching sets of small cruets. Many of them are fashioned of glass to facilitate discerning which vessel holds which liquid. Many come with lids in the shape of a cross. The lids were probably intended to keep impurities out of the water and wine, but often such lids get in the way or cause pointless ceremonial actions to remove and replace them. It is simpler to stow the lids in the sacristy. Cruets are often kept in a small refrigerator in the sacristy for the 467 sake of preserving the wine, but the water does not need to be chilled. The usefulness of cruets has waned with the changing practice of Communion. When only the priest received Communion from the cup, a small amount of wine was needed for Mass. When the Blood of Christ is shared with the faithful, a flagon will probably replace the wine cruet.

105. Traditionally the water cruet has served two purposes. The deacon or priest uses it to pour a little water into the wine during the preparation of the gifts. The server uses it to wash the priest's hands (GIRM 76, 145, 118). However, the American bishops recommend separate water vessels. "A suitable pitcher and basin may be used for the washing of the priest's hands. The water intended to be mixed with the wine should be contained in a smaller, separate vessel appropriate for that purpose." The pitcher and basin for washing hands should allow a generous use of water (IOM 51).

106. A basin is set on the credence table before Mass for the washing of the hands. The GIRM never mentions it by name. It says that "whatever 111 is needed for the washing of hands" is placed on the credence table before Mass (118c) and that the priest washes his hands "as the minister pours the water" (145), but it never says whether the minister pours the water into a vessel. The vessel has often been called a finger bowl, but the American bishops more rightly call for a basin "if the priest is to do more than wet the tips of his fingers" (IOM 51). 496

Cloths

107. Besides the altar cloth, a number of other cloths are used. The corporal is kept at the credence table before Mass (GIRM 118c) and brought 69

to the altar for the preparation of the gifts (73). The GIRM never describes the corporal, but traditionally it is a square white cloth with a red cross stitched in the center, folded in thirds top and bottom and then in thirds side to side. It is opened on the altar in a way that the creases can be refolded inwardly to collect any particles of the consecrated bread and

spilled drops of the consecrated wine. More than one corporal may be used. When concelebrants share Communion, for example, additional corporals may be placed under the consecrated bread and wine (248, 249). When the vessels are cleaned after Communion at the credence table, they

rest on another corporal (183). Logically, if the bread and wine are held in several vessels, more than one corporal will be needed, or one larger one could be made, not necessarily square or foldable into thirds. No specific kind of material is specified for the corporal, but linen is traditional.

108. The GIRM never refers to the burse. The burse was a simple container made of two cardboard squares encased in cloth the color of the

liturgical day. These squares were bound together at one end, open at the other, and joined on the sides by material in accordion folds. Prior to the Second Vatican Council, the folded corporal was tucked inside the burse. Its usage has been discontinued.

109. The pall is a small cloth square stiffened with cardboard or plastic. It is usually white. In the past the priest used the pall to keep the chalice covered after it was filled with wine. The pall kept bugs out. Its use is no longer required but is permitted "if appropriate" (GIRM 118c, 142). The OM includes it among items that are brought to the altar (21) but

never mentions it again. Other references to the pall (GIRM 139, 190, and 306) presume it is in use, but 73 presumes it is not. If multiple chalices are used, it would be logical to use multiple palls, although the GIRM never addresses this issue. Many parish churches omit the pall altogether because it is not needed and because removing and replacing it draws unnecessary attention to its relatively insignificant purpose. But other parishes use one or more palls to keep bugs out. If a pall is to be used, it belongs on the credence table before Mass begins (118c).

110. Purificators are set on the credence table before Mass (GIRM 118c). The GIRM never describes the purificator and gives only a partial account of its use. Traditionally the purificator is a rectangular white cloth with a red cross stitched in the center. If the cloth is laid out with the shorter sides on top and bottom, it is folded left to right in thirds, and then top to bottom in half. Formerly the two flat sides of the purificator were folded

back again partway down from the center fold and parallel to it. This allowed the purificator to ride inside the chalice in the shape of an M, but this is no longer necessary. Purificators may be made of any material, but the traditional linen and cotton are more absorbent than synthetic substances. Paper purificators are never appropriate. Normally, after the priest drinks from the chalice, he wipes the rim with the purificator, but the GIRM does not mention this practice (158, 182). When the Blood of Christ is shared with the assembly, the Communion minister wipes the chalice rim with the purificator after each person drinks (286). After Communion the purificator is used to push particles of consecrated bread from the paten into the chalice (179) and to dry the chalice once it has been cleaned (163). *699*

737

767, 772

111.   Traditionally the priest uses another cloth to dry his hands after the washing. The GIRM recognizes that some items will rest on the credence table before Mass for the washing of the hands (118c), but it does not name them. For the sake of authenticity, a cloth resembling a hand towel should be used (IOM 109). *106, 496*

112.   A veil may cover the chalice. It may be the color of the day or white (GIRM 118). The chalice veil had been used for centuries, but many par- *90* ishes discontinued it after the Second Vatican Council, even though the GIRM of the time said in English, "The chalice should be covered with a veil" (80). But this was an excessive translation of the Latin words, which said, "The chalice may be covered with a veil." Now the GIRM has strengthened the option in Latin, calling it "praiseworthy" (118), but a comparison of the English translations alone makes it appear that the use of the veil has been softened from something that "should" be done to something that is nice to do. These nuances are lost in the IOM, which states that the chalice "is fittingly covered with a veil" (51), as if it were a universal practice. There are problems with a chalice veil. For example, when Communion is distributed under both kinds, multiple chalices may be used. There would be little point in covering the presider's chalice while leaving the others open or in covering all the chalices before Mass. In addition, the stacking of vessels beneath the chalice veil makes little symbolic sense. The GIRM never describes the stack, but traditionally the chalice was set on the table, a purificator folded like the letter M was draped in and over the chalice, the paten rested on top of the purificator, the pall covered the paten, and the veil concealed the entire stack. The corporal was tucked inside a burse and rested on top of the chalice veil. The stack made it handy to carry everything from the sacristy to the

altar, but it disregarded the functions of these elements. When preparing a dinner at home, no one sets the wine glass on the table, covers it with a napkin, places a bread plate on top, covers it with a fly swatter, drapes it all with a veil, and tops it off with a place mat. But these are the functional equivalents of the elements in the traditional stack of vessels. The GIRM calls the use of the chalice veil "praiseworthy," and perhaps it is from a traditional perspective, but it obscures the symbolic purpose of sacred vessels and cloths.

775

Credence table

113. The credence table is a small service table set in the sanctuary. It *419* holds articles put into use throughout the Mass. The purification of ves- *766* sels may take place there after Communion. It may hold items after their use, such as the Book of the Gospels and the vessels and cloths for *353, 776* Communion. The credence table is generally located against a side wall of the sanctuary. In some churches it is a shelf built into the wall. Some parishes keep the credence table next to the altar to save the ministers some steps, but this practice blurs the visual distinction between the credence table and the altar.

114. Before Mass the following items are to be set on the credence table: the chalice, corporal, purificator, the communion-plate for the faithful, and the materials for washing the priest's hands (water pitcher, basin, *496* and towel). The following items may be set on the credence table if desired: the pall, paten, ciboria, the bread, cruets with water and wine, and a vessel of water to be blessed if the sprinkling rite is to occur (GIRM *227* 118c). This allocation of items is practical, though not completely.

a. Regarding the paten, the postconciliar English translation of the GIRM said "a paten and ciboria, if needed" are set on the credence table (80). The revised GIRM reads, "the paten and, if needed, ciboria" are set there, as if the paten is no longer optional. The Latin words did not change: *"patena et pyxides, si necessariae sunt."* The postconciliar English translation is more accurate. No paten is placed on the credence table if all the bread is brought to *437* the altar in another vessel.

b. Regarding the communion-plate, the only other reference to it in the GIRM is to Communion by intinction (287), in which the priest dips the Body of Christ into the Blood of Christ and places the sacred elements directly onto the tongue of the communicant.

The communicant is to hold the communion-plate beneath his or her chin in this instance. As rarely as intinction is practiced, it is puzzling to find the communion-plate listed among the items necessary for the celebration of Mass. After the publication of the GIRM, the CDWDS expressed its preference that the communion-plate be retained "to avoid the danger of the sacred host or some fragment of it falling" (RS 93). Prior to the Second Vatican Council, a server held the communion-plate beneath the chin of everyone receiving the Body of Christ. Communion in the hand had not yet been approved. The use of the communion-plate had been discontinued in many parishes because the extra person and vessel threatened to cause more accidents than they prevented. Still today, people seem capable of avoiding dangers without the communion-plate. *731*

741

c.   Bread and the cruets are set on the credence table "unless all of these are presented by the faithful in procession at the Offertory." But the water cruet should not be presented at that time. It belongs on the credence table before Mass. *425*

d.   If the priest uses a pillow or bookstand to prop up the Missal on the altar, it would logically rest on the credence table before Mass begins. *420*

115.   Most churches place a small table near the door of the church, where the bread and wine are set before Mass begins. Although the practice is widespread, the GIRM makes no mention of it. Gifts may be brought forward (OM 22), but the documents never say from where. The bread and *423, 448* wine set here should be of sufficient quantity for the Communion of the faithful. The GIRM cautions that too much wine should not be prepared (285a), but in courtesy, too little wine should not be prepared either. The GIRM recognizes that the priest may need to consume whatever of the *446* consecrated wine remains after Communion (163), implying that enough should be prepared for the Communion of all the faithful. The faithful *757* will be encouraged to receive Communion from bread consecrated at the very Mass they are attending (85), so enough bread should be set out to avoid the distribution of Communion from previously consecrated breads stored in the tabernacle. *437*

Cross

116.   A cross bearing an image of the crucified Christ should be placed on or near the altar (GIRM 117, 308). Alternatively, such a cross may be

carried in procession and then placed near the altar, "in which case it ought to be the only cross used" (122). If the processional cross serves as the church's crucifix, it is appropriate to station it near the altar even apart from Mass as a reminder of "the saving Passion of the Lord" (308). This image of Christ is directly associated with the altar and with the Mass, so it should be worthy, dignified and beautiful (350; cf. 349).

117. Having the cross on the altar (GIRM 117, 308) is the first option listed. That normally indicates a preference, but in this instance it would not be ideal. Objects placed on the altar should not interfere with the assembly's view of it (307). This option is probably a concession to older churches in which the main altar is still fixed against the back wall, and the crucifix is mounted upon it or above it. This is one of several places where the liturgical documents implicitly sanction the priest's turning his back to the people throughout the celebration of Mass. But the altar should be arranged in a way that the priest can say Mass facing the people (299). A crucifix placed on a freestanding altar and facing the priest would deliver little devotional support for the assembly. Having the crucifix near the altar or mounted on a wall better serves the Eucharist.

Candles

118. Lighted candles should be placed on or near the altar (GIRM 117), unless they will be carried in the entrance procession and placed there (122). Candles symbolize reverence and the festiveness of celebration (307). There is no ceremony in the Catholic liturgy for lighting the candles. Some weddings include a ceremonial lighting of candles before the principal guests are seated, but there is no liturgical rubric governing this practice. Usually the sacristan or servers light candles before the service begins. Many churches prefer to have the candles lit before the faithful enter, because the action of lighting them may be more distracting than it is prayerful.

119. At least two candles should be lit, but four or six may also be used, especially for Sundays and holydays. Seven candles are lit when the diocesan bishop presides (GIRM 117; CB 128). These candles should be arranged harmoniously in a way that does not obstruct the view of the assembly (307). For this reason it is usually best for the candles to stand on the floor, not on the altar (IOM 52). There is nothing improper about lighting three or five candles or even more than seven for Mass; it all depends on how they are arranged in the sanctuary. The guiding

principles are reverence and festivity. To avoid clutter, if a candle is not to be lit, it probably does not belong in the sanctuary.

120. A wax candle or oil lamp is kept alight near the tabernacle "to honor the presence of Christ" (316).

121. The American bishops ask that candles "be made of a substance that gives a living flame and is seen to be consumed in giving its light" (IOM 52). Some churches have replaced votive and altar candles with electrical surrogates. "Electric lights as a substitute for candles are not permitted" (BLS 93). Spring-loaded pillar oil candles that resemble wax candles are 45 not "seen to be consumed" in giving light; they lack genuineness, simulating what they are not, and are best avoided (cf. GIRM 292).

122. Formerly candles were required to be 51 percent beeswax, but this is no longer true. Beeswax candles burn without the noxious fumes associated with some non-natural substitutes. They fit the criterion of worthiness that applies to everything used at Mass (GIRM 348) and the "concern for genuineness of materials" (292), but other substances are permitted, especially in parts of the world where beeswax is hard to obtain.

Flowers

123. Flowers contribute to the reverence and festivity of the Eucharist. They may be placed around the altar, but not upon it (GIRM 305). The quantity of flowers should relate to the feast or season. During Advent, for example, flowers should be used with moderation; during Lent, they are forbidden, except on solemnities and feasts. Some parishes decorate for Lent with dried flowers, cacti or bare branches.

124. The GIRM promotes the use of flowers on the Fourth Sunday of Lent (305), when rose vestments may be worn. Traditionally the day signals the 90 faithful that this rigorous season is half over. However, the Fourth Sunday of Lent is also the second of three consecutive Sundays when scrutinies are celebrated for the elect before their baptism at Easter. In that context there is little cause for more festivity on that particular Sunday.

125. Children may be involved in preparing the place and the altar with its ornamentation (DMC 22, 29). If flowers are to be arranged, children may assist. 427

126. In general, the decoration of the church should contribute to noble simplicity, not ostentation, in accordance with artistic principles (GIRM

292, 325, 351). Genuine materials are better than artificial ones, "to foster the instruction of the faithful and the dignity of the entire sacred place" (292). For example, real flowers are more worthy than fake ones. "The use of living flowers and plants, rather than artificial greens, serves as a reminder of the gift of life God has given to the human community" (BLS 129). In whatever region the church is located, the artistic styles of the area have a place "in keeping with the culture and traditions of each people" (325).

Tabernacle

127. The tabernacle is the place where previously consecrated Communion breads are reserved. The Body of Christ is kept in a fixture suggestive of its contents, primarily to facilitate bringing Communion to the sick throughout the week. The tabernacle is also a place for private adoration by the faithful. Many churches still retrieve from the tabernacle Communion breads to be distributed to some of the faithful at every Mass, but this practice is discouraged (GIRM 85).

663

128. The tabernacle should be located "in a part of the church that is truly noble, prominent, readily visible, beautifully decorated, and suitable for prayer" (GIRM 314). That place may be in the sanctuary, preferably not on the altar, or it may be "in some chapel suitable for the faithful's private adoration and prayer and organically connected to the church and readily visible to the Christian faithful" (315). "The location also should allow for easy access by people in wheelchairs and by those who have other disabilities" (BLS 74). For many centuries the tabernacle occupied a central position against the back wall atop the altar. In some churches it still remains in the center against the back wall (cf. GIRM 310). However, the placement of the tabernacle outside the sanctuary helps focus the attention of the faithful upon the altar (cf. 299) and provides a separate area for private worship, so that the nave remains oriented toward public worship. The GIRM argues that keeping the tabernacle off the top of the altar "is more in keeping with the meaning of the sign" (315). The same could be said for its placement apart from the sanctuary.

45

171, 763

Other Objects

129. Images of Jesus, Mary, and the saints "should be displayed for veneration by the faithful," but their number should not be increased indiscriminately, and there should be only one image of any particular

saint (GIRM 318). "Provision should be made for the devotion of the entire community," but the arrangement of images should not "distract the faithful's attention from the celebration itself." Many Catholics pray before the image of a saint before Mass begins. Others are inspired by the example of the saints upon whose images they gaze during the celebration of Mass. But the fundamental orientation of the church is toward the altar (299).

45

130. Microphones may also stand in the sanctuary, but they "should be arranged discreetly" (GIRM 306). Many priests wear wireless microphones, eliminating the need for a standing microphone at the chair. The focus should be on the principal furnishings, not on the microphones. The entire sound system should be balanced with the acoustics of the room. 147

131. In the sacristy the vestments are prepared, together with items that may be needed for the procession: the Book of the Gospels, incense, cross, and candles (GIRM 119). Traditionally the sacristy was located adjacent 151 to the sanctuary. But a change has happened since the Second Vatican Council. With the broader participation of the faithful, the entrance procession usually moves through their midst. It has become more common for a vesting sacristy to be located near the door of the church, so that the procession of ministers naturally moves through the assembly. "If the vesting sacristy is located in the rear of the church, it is helpful to have an additional work sacristy that offers easy access to the altar located near the sanctuary" (BLS 234). 764, 776, 828

132. The diocesan bishop consults with "the diocesan commission on the sacred Liturgy and sacred Art" concerning the construction, restoration, and remodeling of sacred buildings (GIRM 291). The bishop "must promote, regulate, and be vigilant over the liturgical life in his diocese" (387). Many particulars for the arrangement of church buildings are established by diocesan policy.

ENTRANCE CHANT

The Song

133. The entrance chant is the text sung while the priest and ministers go to the altar (OM 1). It opens the celebration, fosters the unity of the assembly, introduces the mystery of the season or the day, and accompanies the procession (GIRM 47, 121).

134. The people may sing alone, or they may alternate parts of the chant with the choir or a cantor (GIRM 48). The choir may also sing alone (48), but if the music is to foster the unity of the assembly (cf. 47), it is best if *148* all are invited to sing at least part of the song.

135. In practice, the entrance chant goes by other names. It is often called the opening hymn or song. Many people know it by its Latin title, the introit.

136. A text for the entrance chant appears in the Missal for every day of the Church year, but another song may replace it. In the United States there are four musical options (GIRM 48). The first is "the antiphon from the *Roman Missal* or the Psalm from the *Roman Gradual* as set to music there or in another musical setting." The Missal's antiphon is the text of the entrance chant. The Missal does not include musical notation for it. The word "antiphon" presumes that the text serves as a refrain that alternates with verses, but no verses appear in the Missal. A verse is given, however, in the Roman Gradual, a book unknown to most parishes. The *Graduale Romanum* contains Gregorian chant notation for the sung texts of the Mass. Its entrance chants, for example, assign musical notation to the text that appears in the Missal and for a versicle not appearing in the Missal, drawn from a psalm. The antiphon is to be sung before and after the versicle, making it more of an antiphon than the Missal leads one to realize. The American edition of the GIRM errs mildly, therefore, when it says the first option is either the antiphon from the Missal or the psalm from the Gradual—the antiphon appears in both places. The IOM similarly misstates the first choice as "an antiphon and psalm from the *Roman Missal* as set to music by the *Roman Gradual*" (67). The antiphon alone appears in the Missal; it also appears in the Gradual with one line from one psalm. The first option, then, is any musical setting of the words that appear as the entrance chant for the day, *410, 703* with or without the line of the psalm following it in the Roman Gradual.

137. The second option for music is "the seasonal antiphon and Psalm of the *Simple Gradual*" (GIRM 48). This is another book largely unknown to parishes, except for those using a resource such as Paul F. Ford's *By Flowing Waters*. The *Graduale Simplex* contains a simple setting of chants for use throughout the year. Instead of offering new chants for each day, it gives fewer chants that may be repeated throughout a season. For the thirty-four weeks in Ordinary Time, for example, there are a total of eight options for the entrance chant (and for other parts of the Mass). Here, though, the antiphon alternates with up to ten short verses of a psalm.

The second option, then, is any musical setting of a prescribed seasonal text with multiple psalm verses as found in the Simple Gradual.

138. The third musical option for the entrance chant in the United States is "a song from another collection of psalms and antiphons, approved by the Conference of Bishops or the diocesan Bishop, including psalms arranged in responsorial or metrical forms" (GIRM 48). This option broadens the scope beyond the texts that appear in the liturgical books, while recommending musical settings of their primary source: the Book of Psalms.

139. Finally, the option frequently taken by many parishes in the United States is "a suitable liturgical song similarly approved by the Conference of Bishops or the diocesan Bishop" (GIRM 48). This option allows singing from the broadest repertoire of liturgical music. It would not support the singing of secular love songs at weddings. When choosing the text and music for the entrance chant, the appropriate song will be one that helps introduce the thoughts of the faithful "to the mystery of the liturgical season or festivity" (47).

140. The approval of local bishops in the third and fourth options can be formal, but commonly bishops have given at least tacit approval to the use of songs appearing in published worship aids, if not songs composed by local musicians. In 1996 the Bishops' Committee on the Liturgy said of music in the United States, "No official approbation is required for hymns, songs, and acclamations written for the assembly,* provided they are not sung settings of the liturgical texts of the Order of Mass" (*Committee on the Liturgy Newsletter* 33 [January/February 1997] 5). Nonetheless, the GIRM gives conferences of bishops and diocesan bishops the authority to restrict the music to be sung in parishes. It is hard to imagine a conference of bishops ratifying the contents of a hymnal song by song, culture by culture, but they have the authority to do so.

141. Singing is of great importance to the celebration of the Mass (GIRM 40). This is especially true of the dialogues between the priest and people on Sundays and holy days of obligation and of music, such as the entrance chant, sung by the priest and people together. The Second Vatican Council called for the conscious, active, and fruitful participation of the faithful in the liturgy (SC 11). Singing is one of the most important ways to achieve it. Singing "is to be especially encouraged in every way for Masses celebrated with children, in view of their special affinity for music" (DMC 30). Conferences of bishops may permit the use of recorded

* *Appendix to the General Instruction of the Roman Missal*, number 19.

music at Masses with children (DMC 32). Normally, though, the use of prerecorded accompaniments or solos should be avoided. The music of the liturgy needs "living, acting people entering into communion with mystery" (*Notitiae* 3 [1967] 3–4).

142. Mass may be celebrated without singing, but music is "appropriate, whenever possible" (GIRM 115).

143. In actual practice, some people do not sing. Many do not even pick up a hymnal. Given the importance of singing at Mass, the refusal of many members of the assembly to sing is a more serious problem than is commonly admitted. If one purpose of the entrance chant, for example, is to "foster the unity of those who have been gathered," non-participation in song may unintentionally signal disunity. In a culture where people listen to recorded music more than they sing—even their own national anthem—amateurs may feel ashamed to try what professionals do. Presiders and participants with little or no skill at singing can still lend whatever voice they have. Surely God is more pleased when people are caught up in song regardless of their skill than when they withdraw from it altogether.

Leading the Song

144. The entrance chant may be led by a cantor or choir, who "lead and sustain the people's singing" (GIRM 104). The cantor may serve as the psalmist (LM 22; IOM 18), but these roles may also be distinct. A cantor may lead the singing from some visible place such as a cantor stand, but not the ambo (LM 33).

58

145. In many parishes the cantor announces the song that opens the service. Consequently, this is often the first voice that speaks to the entire assembly. The American bishops urge that people be "made welcome by representatives of the community and acknowledged informally by their neighbors" (IOM 23). It would be courteous if the cantor's first words were a greeting such as "Good morning." In some communities, the cantor invites the faithful to stand and greet those around them. This gives people permission to extend friendly greetings to those nearby with whom they will sing, pray, hear the word of God, and share Communion. It honors the silence that precedes the start of the Mass (GIRM 45) and serves a function separate from the sign of peace, which is part of the symbolism that specifically prepares for Communion. It allows a stranger to be welcomed and for the people to enter the first song as one.

56

633

146. If the cantor announces the hymn, words such as "Please join in singing. . ." are more appropriate than "Join me in singing," which sounds as though the song belongs to the cantor, or "Let us greet our celebrant," which sounds as though the song is about the priest. The liturgical documents do not call for any text here, so each community determines the words that best capture its spirit and the intention of the entrance chant. Some communities avoid the announcement altogether by printing a weekly worship aid or posting numbers on a hymn board.

147. Some cantors use the microphone even while the people are singing. However, the amplification of one voice makes it hard for the assembly to hear its own voice. Cantors may need the microphone to make announcements or sing a solo, but the assembly usually sings its parts better if the cantor has stepped away or switched off the microphone. *130*

Other Matters

148. The entrance chant may be recited (GIRM 48). All the faithful, some of them, or a lector may recite the antiphon from the Missal (48, 198). If necessary, the priest may do it. There is no provision for omitting the entrance chant, even though this happens in some parishes. Even when the text is recited, it serves its function best when it accompanies the procession of the ministers to the altar. In some places the priest leads the spoken text after he reaches the chair, but ideally the antiphon accompanies the procession (47). *134*

149. If the entrance chant is not sung, the priest may "adapt it as an introductory explanation" (GIRM 48; IOM 65). The best occasion for this *209* option is after the greeting (IOM 67; cf. GIRM 31) rather than during the procession.

150. Everyone stands at the beginning of the entrance chant (GIRM 43). Of course, those who are infirm may remain seated.

151. If incense is used, the charcoal should be lit several minutes before Mass begins. Just before the procession, the priest puts incense on top *131* of the hot coals in the thurible, and he blesses it with the sign of the cross (GIRM 120, 277). A deacon may assist (173); the GIRM does not say how, but traditionally he holds the boat, opens it while the priest spoons incense from it to the thurible, and closes it after the priest replaces the spoon. Alternatively, the deacon may hold both the thurible and the boat, especially if there is no thurifer. In this case he first hands the priest the

boat, then lifts the thurible while the priest spoons incense into it. The
deacon then takes the boat from the priest.

152. The priest says nothing during these actions (GIRM 120, 277). Prior
to the Second Vatican Council, he addressed the incense while making
the sign of the cross: "May you be blessed by him in whose honor you
will be burned," but this practice has been discontinued.

153. Incensation is "an expression of reverence and of prayer" (GIRM
276). Incense may be used in any form of Mass (276), but it usually indicates a celebration of importance (49, 211), for example Sundays and
festive days (119). Some people have allergies to incense; some parishes
publish the schedule of Masses with and without incense in the bulletin
or on their website.

PROCESSION

ORDER OF PROCESSION

154. The procession of ministers moves to the altar (OM 1). The order
of procession is as follows: incense, cross and candles, other ministers,
lector, deacon, and priest (GIRM 120, 172).

155. Most parishes use altar servers to exercise the duties of instituted
acolytes, except to distribute Communion and purify vessels (GIRM 98,
191–192). Usually altar servers are children, but adults may fill this role.
The GIRM anticipates the potential misunderstanding of the word "acolyte" by stressing that the one who may assist the priest in giving Communion is "a duly instituted acolyte" (191). The CDWDS says GIRM 187–190,
193; 101, 194–198 refer to acolytes and lectors "by temporary deputation"
(RS 44), though this is not at all clear in the GIRM. The CDWDS admits
that "girls or women may also be admitted to this service of the altar" but
says "it is altogether laudable to maintain the noble custom by which boys
or youths, customarily termed servers, provide service of the altar" (RS
47). In today's culture many parishes would find it offensive, not noble,
to exclude girls and restrict this service at the altar to boys.

156. Because the GIRM evolved from elaborate ceremonies involving
ordained clergy and instituted ministers, it still prefers to divide most
responsibilities among them. Altar servers and other deputed lay ministers may perform many liturgical actions "in the absence of an instituted
acolyte" (100). This sentence makes it appear that altar servers are the

exception rather than the rule, but the contrary is true in almost all parishes. Consequently, the GIRM does not give a clear list of guidelines for altar servers, who are among the most common ministers in parish Masses. This frustrates the uniformity of ceremonies, but it also allows some flexibility in an otherwise scrupulous document. The IOM addresses the situation with a paragraph summarizing the responsibilities of servers—when they process and what they hold (22). The diocesan bishop may establish norms for servers and other ministers (GIRM 107, 387).

157. The word "server" occurs only three times in the English translation of the GIRM. Servers may carry candles in the gospel procession (175), they may ring a bell and perform incensations during the Eucharistic Prayer (150); and they should be suitably vested (339). However, the Latin word in all three of these passages is *minister*, a word translated with the English cognate "minister" in dozens of other places throughout the GIRM. The translators apparently attempted to specify certain actions an altar server might perform at the Mass, but these incomplete distinctions do not derive from the source. *337*
564, 572,
582, 94

158. If incense is used, the person carrying it—the thurifer—leads the procession (GIRM 120a, 276a). The thurifer usually holds the thurible by the end of the chain and lets it swing gently to one side as he or she walks toward the altar.

159. Ministers carry lighted candles, and an acolyte or another minister carries a cross between them (GIRM 120b, 188). The image on the cross faces front (CB 128). If no incense is used, these ministers lead the procession. Traditionally there are two lighted candles in the procession, but more could be used; the GIRM does not specify how many. The CB suggests seven, the number of altar candles recommended for Mass with a bishop (128). Altar servers usually perform this function. *116*

160. "The acolytes and other ministers" follow (GIRM 120c), although it is not clear who these are. The GIRM probably has in mind installed acolytes (98), ministers not generally present in parish celebrations. But "other ministers" are probably non-installed assistants, such as servers. In the parish any other ministers could join the procession at this point. BLS permits the use of processional banners (127); logically, some ministers could carry them in the entrance procession.

161. Some parishes place their Communion ministers in the entrance procession, and GIRM 120c can be read to tolerate the practice. But ministers who process are usually headed toward the sanctuary, not the

nave. Communion ministers more appropriately sit with their family and other members of the assembly until their time of service. The entrance procession is not listed among the actions of Communion ministers in the United States (IOM 21).

47, 756, 824

162. The DMC allows children to join the entrance procession (34), but it does not specify at which point. Placing them among the "other ministers" of GIRM 120c would honor the order of procession. On special occasions the procession at this point might logically include children celebrating First Communion; a couple on their wedding anniversary; or parents, godparents and infants to be baptized. Ushers may assist with this procession by helping keep order (IOM 23).

163. A lector comes next in procession (GIRM 120d). If there is no deacon, the lector may carry the Book of the Gospels. The lector holds the book "slightly elevated." In some places, especially in large churches, the lector might hold the book high above his or her head, but the GIRM avoids recommending the practice. Some lectors cannot physically perform this action. The principle is to draw attention to the book, not to the lector, and to hold the book with dignity, neither ostentatiously nor carelessly. The lector wears "approved attire" (194), but this refers to instituted lec-

93

tors (99). If the Book of the Gospels is already on the altar (117) or if the parish has no Book of the Gospels, a lector may still process without it. But the procession is to give attention to the book.

164. The 2002 GIRM clarified that the Lectionary is not to be carried in procession (120d). This had become a common practice in parishes. The gospel has special significance among the readings at Mass, as becomes especially obvious in the moments preceding its proclamation. The dis-

322–348

tinctiveness of the gospels is anticipated early in the service by having the book that contains them carried in procession and placed upon the altar. The gospels containing the words of Christ are to be placed upon the altar signifying Christ (298), thus unifying two primary symbols of

65

the Liturgy of the Word and the Liturgy of the Eucharist. In the course of the Mass, the altar and the Book of the Gospels are the only objects

179, 351

kissed by the deacon and priest (273).

165. If there is a deacon, he enters alongside the priest (GIRM 172). Or he may walk immediately in front of the priest, carrying the Book of the Gospels, slightly elevated. The deacon "holds first place among those who minister in the Eucharistic Celebration" (94). He may exercise his ministry at any Mass (116).

166. The priest who celebrates the Mass comes last in the procession (GIRM 120e). He offers the sacrifice in the person of Christ, stands at the head of the faithful, presides over their prayer, proclaims salvation to them, associates them with himself in offering the sacrifice, and shares Communion (93).

167. One minister may serve as a master of ceremonies (GIRM 106). This minister may help plan the liturgy and oversee the actions of other ministers during the Mass. The master of ceremonies need not process in with the other ministers. He or she may help pace the ministers down the aisle or direct them to places from the sanctuary.

168. The American bishops allow postponing the procession on those Sundays when the rite of blessing and sprinkling of water replaces the act of penitence (IOM 74). In this case a brief entrance chant would suffice   *229* at the beginning. Then the priest makes the sign of the cross and greets the people from the door of the church. At the door he blesses the water and combines the sprinkling of the assembly with his procession to the altar. In larger churches this saves some steps. The Missal, however, calls for the priest to start this ritual from the chair (RM Appendix 2:2).

Reverencing the Altar

Bows and Genuflections

169. "When they reach the sanctuary," the ministers reverence the altar with a profound bow (GIRM 49). But OM 1 and GIRM 122 say the bow is made when they reach the *altar*. At some Masses the ministers enter from a sacristy adjacent to the sanctuary, not up the middle aisle. In those circumstances, if they reverenced the altar "when they reach the sanctuary," it would happen ridiculously at the door of the sacristy. In this case they appropriately make their reverence when they reach the altar. The OM does not seem to envision an entrance procession up the aisle, which is quite common in parishes.

170. All ministers in the procession make a profound bow to the altar (OM 1; GIRM 49, 122), but there are exceptions. A deacon or lector processing with the Book of the Gospels directly enters the sanctuary without making any sign of reverence (GIRM 173, 195). Those carrying cross and candles   *163, 165* will find it difficult to execute a profound bow; a bow of the head would be more practical. Perhaps it is an oversight, but the GIRM only calls for these ministers to bow their heads as an alternative to genuflecting (274).   *172*

171. If the tabernacle is located "in the sanctuary," the ministers genuflect when they approach the altar (GIRM 274); otherwise they do not. The IOM says they genuflect if the tabernacle is "behind or near the altar" (68), but that is not precisely what the GIRM says. Sanctuary design varies somewhat from church to church. One tabernacle might be near the altar but out of the sanctuary. Catholics feel an intense devotion toward the tabernacle, as well they should, because it contains the Blessed Sacrament. Still, the point of the Mass is to participate at the miracle that will take place on the altar, not to exercise devotions to the reserved Blessed Sacrament. When the tabernacle is outside the sanctuary, the entrance procession for the Mass rightly gives its full attention to the altar.

172. Ministers carrying the cross or candles do not genuflect if the tabernacle is in the sanctuary. They bow their heads instead (GIRM 274). Those carrying candles need to be especially cautious of the flame and hot wax. A deacon or lector carrying the Book of the Gospels makes no genuflection (173, 195).

173. The GIRM does not say that the genuflection or bow of the head to the tabernacle replaces the profound bow to the altar. Some might argue that the genuflection should replace the bow to simplify the marks of reverence in the sanctuary; after all, the priest and deacon will shortly bend down to kiss the altar. Others might say that the actions are distinct and show signs of respect to different objects in the sanctuary. Some of those might hold that the genuflection should come first, in recognition of the Blessed Sacrament before the Mass continues. Others might prefer that the bow come first because the altar is more significant for the celebration of Mass. There is no ruling on this matter, and the practice will vary from church to church, depending on the design of the sanctuary and local customs.

174. In some parishes the ministers process down the aisle but wait at the edge of the sanctuary for the priest to arrive. Then they all make the reverence together before entering the sanctuary. However, ministers make their reverence "when they reach the sanctuary" (GIRM 49) or "on reaching the altar" (122). This suggests that each minister processes in, makes the reverence, and takes his or her place without awaiting the priest.

Placement of Objects

175. The crossbearer sets the cross upright next to the altar if there is no other cross in the sanctuary (GIRM 122, 188). Otherwise he or she places it in some dignified place, such as a designated spot in the working sacristy.

176. Those carrying candles place them on the altar or near it (GIRM 122), being careful not to obstruct the assembly's view (GIRM 307; IOM 52).   *118*

177. The lector or deacon carrying the Book of the Gospels moves directly from the aisle into the sanctuary up to the altar without making any sign of reverence (GIRM 173, 195) and places the book on the altar. Some think   *170, 172* it looks better if this minister walks around the altar and sets the book down while facing the assembly. Others prefer to have the minister set the book down without circling the altar. In some parishes the minister sets the book flat. In other parishes the minister stands the book up by opening it slightly, but such a precariously placed book may topple over. In still other parishes the minister sets the book in a stand prearranged on the altar before Mass. A stand holds the book upright so that the faithful   *71, 340* may more easily see it. The GIRM is silent on these matters.

178. If the lector is the minister who places the book on the altar, it would be proper for him or her to make a profound bow to the altar upon leaving the sanctuary before taking a place in the nave (CB 72). If the deacon is the minister who places the book on the altar, he may remain in the sanctuary to kiss the altar with the priest (GIRM 173).

Kissing the Altar

179. When the priest approaches the altar, he kisses it (OM 1; GIRM 49, 123, 173). The deacon does the same (GIRM 49, 173). The GIRM does not say whether or not they do this facing the people. In many churches it will appear more polite for them to walk behind the altar and kiss the top near the center of the edge where most of the action of the Mass will take place. Relics are stored there in some altars, but the veneration is to the altar, not to the relics. Among cultures where kissing the altar would offend traditions of the region, their conference of bishops may establish some other sign of veneration, with the consent of the Apostolic See (273).   *823*

Incensing the Cross and the Altar

180. The priest may then incense the cross and the altar (OM 1; GIRM 49, 123, 276b). The deacon may help the priest put incense into the thurible (GIRM 173), but this hardly seems necessary if incense was added at the beginning of the entrance procession.   *151*

181. The objects to be incensed here are consistently listed as "cross and altar" (OM 1; GIRM 49, 123, 276b). The incensation of the cross at this

time was omitted after Vatican II, but the 2002 Missal restored it. The practice had been traditional at solemn Masses. At the time, the cross was traditionally situated above the altar against the back wall. It used to be incensed first with three single swings of the thurible.

182. The priest incenses the cross first if it is situated on or near the altar (GIRM 277). He makes a profound bow before the cross, swings the thurible three times toward the cross, and bows again. Then he bows to the altar, incenses it by walking around it with a series of single swings (123, 277), and bows to it again.

183. If the cross is located somewhat apart from the altar, the priest first incenses the altar by walking around it, and he incenses the cross when he passes in front of it. He makes a profound bow before and after incensing each object (GIRM 277).

116

184. The deacon also assists in incensing. The GIRM does not say how (173), but traditionally the deacon holds the chasuble out of the way of the swinging thurible so that the vestment does not catch fire. The danger is small, and the deacon's traditional role here may be more obtrusive than helpful. Alternatively, the deacon holds the thurible, especially if there is no thurifer. In this case he hands it to the priest and takes it back after the incensations are complete.

185. The GIRM also explains how to incense in circumstances where the altar is still against the wall of a church (277b)—going first to the right and then to the left. But altars are preferably freestanding (299).

52

186. The thurible and boat are usually placed in a stand either in the sanctuary near the seat for the thurifer or in a working sacristy nearby. The documents state no preference. The stand usually suspends the bowl of the smoking thurible off the floor and provides a small shelf near the top for the boat. It should be located where ministers are not likely to knock it over. Some members of the assembly are bound to complain about the smoke. In some parish churches, especially those not well ventilated, the incense stand is kept outdoors.

153

Going to Seats

187. The priest and the ministers go to their seats in the sanctuary (OM 1; GIRM 124, 174, 294). In most parish churches the priest, deacon, and servers sit there.

75

188. The deacon should sit near the priest (GIRM 174, 310). The seating for other ministers should distinguish them from the clergy but enable them to carry out their responsibilities (310). In practice, altar servers who are children cannot pay full attention to the Mass at all times. Seating them where they are not in full view of the assembly will remove some distraction and help the faithful concentrate on the sacred actions of the Mass. Some parishes seat servers just outside the sanctuary, especially if its area is small.

189. The GIRM recommends sanctuary seating for the lector (195) and acolyte (188), but these paragraphs refer to men instituted into these ministries by a bishop (cf. 98–99), even though RS 44 says they also refer to non-instituted lay ministers. In most parishes the lector is a layperson *94, 155* who sits in the nave, and the duties of the acolyte are divided between altar servers and Communion ministers, who sit in the sanctuary and the nave respectively. *93*

190. If other ministers have joined the procession, they take their seats in the sanctuary or the nave as appropriate.

SIGN OF THE CROSS

191. At the conclusion of the entrance chant, everyone makes the sign *133* of the cross. Meanwhile the priest says the words, and all the faithful answer, "Amen" (OM 1; GIRM 50, 124).

192. All stand at their places (GIRM 43). The priest should be at the chair. *150* Although some priests go to the altar and read from the Missal lying there, a priest's proper place for the introductory rites is the chair, the place of his presiding. He goes to the altar for the Liturgy of the Eucharist. *75, 457*

193. If the priest wears a wireless microphone, he switches it on. Such a microphone is prudently left off during the opening song.

194. Some priests add the "Amen" before the people can make their response. But that word belongs to the people. This text should be a dialogue in which the people answer, "Amen."

195. The OM provides notes for singing the sign of the cross, because it encourages the singing of dialogues (GIRM 40). A simpler tone is given *141*

in the Missal's first appendix. This music is rarely sung in a typical parish Mass.

196. The documents do not describe how the sign of the cross is made. Traditionally in the Roman Rite, the fingers of the right hand touch the forehead and then the breast as the Father and Son are named, and then the left and right shoulders as the Holy Spirit is named. In some cultures people kiss the thumb of the right hand to conclude this acclamation; others simply fold their hands. Left-handed people may use their left hand.

197. Throughout Mass the head should bow at the name of the Trinity (275a). The GIRM does not say if this pertains to the head of the one naming the Trinity or to everyone. It probably means the one speaking, but it would be fitting for all to bow their heads while making the sign of the cross.

198. OM 1 says the priest should be facing the people. Prior to the Second Vatican Council, the priest made the sign of the cross at the altar with his back to the people, but now he is at the chair. This rubrical reminder to face the people is unnecessary if the chair is properly situated (GIRM 310).

199. Many priests have the opening lines of the Mass memorized and do not need to read from the Missal. Others want the Missal in front of them from the start. Traditionally a server holds the Missal for the priest (IOM 22), preferably in a way that the priest can read the words but still maintain eye contact with the people. The GIRM assigns this task to the acolyte (189). In the absence of other ministers, a deacon seated next to the priest could assist (174). The priest or another minister usually opens the book to a place marked before Mass with a ribbon.

GREETING

200. The priest greets the people using one of three different formulas (e.g., "The Lord be with you"), and the people respond (OM 2; GIRM 50, 124).

201. Some priests substitute or append a more colloquial greeting, such as "Good morning." But the ritual greeting has a deeper significance than a polite hello. The greeting "signifies the presence of the Lord to the community gathered there" (GIRM 50). It would be polite for a cantor or song leader to say "Good morning" before the entrance procession, but the priest uses a more formal greeting.

202. The priest extends his hands while saying this text (OM 2; GIRM 124). Prior to the Council, he used a stylized gesture: palms facing each other, fingers closed, pointed up and not raised above the shoulder; he drew his hands briefly apart, the width of his shoulders, and back again. No such restrictions now apply. Priests generally use a more natural gesture here: arms extended forward, palms up, raising their hands in a gesture of acclamation, welcome, and good will. A good presider will make eye contact with the assembly while saying this text. These are the first words he addresses directly to the people.

263, 503, 539, 631, 802

203. The people's response does not call for any kind of gesture (OM 2), but some people naturally imitate the presider's gesture, as they make eye contact with him and speak to him for the first time in the liturgy.

204. The Missal provides notes for singing this dialogue (OM 2; Appendix I), and the GIRM recommends that such dialogues be sung (40), but this is rarely practiced.

141

INTRODUCTION

205. The priest, a deacon, or another minister may briefly introduce the people to the Mass of the day (OM 3; GIRM 31, 50, 124).

206. Many parishes omit this or have the cantor announce the Mass of the day in conjunction with the opening hymn. But an introduction at this point will help people turn their attention to the significance of the day's gathering.

145

CONTENT

207. The words should be brief (GIRM 31). At a few Masses, such as on Palm Sunday, the Missal scripts a suggested introduction. The priest may adapt these texts "somewhat" to aid the understanding of the assembly. "However, he should always take care to keep to the sense of the text given in the Missal and to express it succinctly."

208. During the introduction "strangers, guests and special groups may briefly be welcomed" (IOM 70). Part of the introduction may directly address any children present (DMC 17) to help them feel included in the celebration. The announcement might also inform people about a second collection, a special blessing to be given later, or the nature of the feast or season being celebrated. Some presiders do this before the sign

of the cross, but waiting until this point allows the greeting to fulfill its function as the first words the priest directs to the people.

209. The content may also spring from the text of the entrance chant in the Missal for the Mass of the day (IOM 65, 67). The antiphon may supply a theme for the opening remarks. If an opening hymn has not been sung, the entrance chant need not be recited before the sign of the cross; it may be incorporated into comments at this point (GIRM 48).

Minister

210. Following the principle that all "should carry out solely but completely that which pertains to them" (GIRM 91), it seems appropriate that the introduction to the Mass be made by a minister other than the priest. The OM equally permits a priest, deacon, or lay minister to give it (3). The GIRM usually permits a lay minister (50, 105b, 124) or encourages a deacon (50, 171d) to speak. Other references to the introduction mention only the priest as its minister (31, 48). The IOM, then, too strongly states that "the introduction is normally the function of the priest," but "on occasion it may be fitting for the deacon or some other member of the congregation to do this" (70).

Location

211. The location from which the introduction is made depends on the minister who delivers it. A priest or deacon speaks from his chair. A lay minister speaks from the cantor stand or another visible place in front, but not from the ambo (LM 33).

ACT OF PENITENCE

212. In the act of penitence the entire assembly carries out a formula of general confession (OM 4; GIRM 51, 125). It begins when the priest gives an introduction and all observe a brief silence.

213. The priest invites everyone, including himself, to acknowledge their sins. Ever since the Council, the English-language Sacramentary has permitted the priest to use his own words, even though the Latin original did not. The current Latin edition of the Missal similarly does not indicate "these or similar words" (OM 4), but the USCCB requested the inclusion of that phrase in the English translation of the Missal, together with two

more sample introductions as had appeared in the Sacramentary. The IOM says the priest uses his own words "where this is foreseen by the rubrics" (71).

214. The OM provides notes for the priest to sing this introduction (4), in accordance with the preference for dialogues to be sung (GIRM 40). *141*

215. All observe a brief silence (OM 4; GIRM 45, 51). During this time the faithful are invited personally to acknowledge their sins in order to enter the celebration with a humble spirit.

216. The act of penitence then takes one of three forms. In the first, all recite the *Confiteor* together (OM 4). The prayer calls for two gestures: all strike their breast as they acknowledge their own fault and bow their head at the mention of Mary's name (GIRM 275a). In practice, few people *603* observe all the bows that 275a calls for.

217. In the second form of the act of penitence, the priest leads the people in a short dialogue of psalm verses (OM 5). Although these texts are eloquent, many Sunday congregations have never learned them.

218. The OM provides notes for the priest and people to sing (5), in accordance with the preference for dialogues to be sung (GIRM 40). *141*

219. In the third form, three invocations are made to Christ, and the people cry out for mercy (OM 6). Seven examples requested by the USCCB for the English-language Missal do not appear in the Latin original. All the invocations appearing in the Missal are samples; others may be freely composed. However, they should be acclamations to Christ who is merciful, not a litany of sins for which the faithful seek mercy. The minister who leads these three acclamations may be the priest, the deacon, or a lay minister. In most parishes the priest or deacon leads them, but a cantor, lector, or commentator could do so as well.

220. If the deacon leads the invocations, a server may hold the Missal for him (GIRM 189), but these texts are often improvised or memorized. Freely composed texts may be prepared beforehand and inserted into a binder held by the minister who leads the invocations or one who assists. *88*

221. The priest then gives an absolution (OM 4, 5, 6; GIRM 51). All answer, "Amen." Even though the OM calls this "absolution," the GIRM points out that it "lacks the efficacy of the Sacrament of Penance." Still, it is a prayer asking forgiveness. *351*

222. The OM provides notes for the priest and people to sing (4, 5, 6),

in accordance with the preference that dialogues be sung (GIRM 40).

223. The invocations of the *Kyrie* follow, unless they were already incorporated into the act of penitence (OM 7; GIRM 52, 125). This seems to refer to the third formula only, meaning that the *Kyrie* follows the first or second formula.

224. The OM gives notes for singing the *Kyrie* (OM 7) and refers to the Roman Gradual for additional versions of this traditional chant. It may be sung by all or in alternation between a cantor or choir and the people. Each acclamation is made twice, but in musical versions it may be repeated more (GIRM 52). *Liturgiam authenticam,* the 2001 instruction on vernacular translations from the CDWDS, says, "Whenever the . . . liturgical text preserves words taken from other ancient languages [the *Kyrie* is in Greek] . . . consideration should be given to preserving the same words in the new vernacular translation, at least as one option among others" (23). Hence it would be appropriate for congregations to learn a setting of the *Kyrie* in Greek as one option in their repertoire of music for the act of penitence.

225. The GIRM does not permit substituting other chants for those found in the OM (366), but this is rarely a problem with the *Kyrie,* which explicitly allows the insertion of tropes to amplify each acclamation (52).

226. In Masses with children the entire act of penitence may be omitted
or expanded according to the needs of participants (DMC 40).

BLESSING AND SPRINKLING OF WATER

227. The blessing and sprinkling of water may replace the act of penitence on Sundays as a reminder of baptism (OM 4n; GIRM 51; IOM 74). This is especially recommended for the Easter season, though perhaps not on Easter Sunday. After the Second Vatican Council, the American Sacramentary replaced the Creed with a renewal of baptismal promises and a sprinkling of water on Easter Day. On such an occasion it would needlessly duplicate the symbol to replace the act of penitence with sprinkling. The rite may be used on other Sundays. Many parishes exercise this option on the Solemnity of the Baptism of the Lord, for example.

228. For the ritual, the priest invites the people to pray, all pray silently, the priest prays aloud, sprinkles the people, and concludes with another

spoken prayer. The rite appears in Appendix II in the Latin edition of the Missal, but the American bishops requested its incorporation into the body of options for the act of penitence in the Order of Mass.

229. The priest should be standing at the chair with a vessel of water nearby (RM Appendix 2:2). The Missal says he turns to the people, but this directive is unnecessary if the chair is properly located in the sanctuary (GIRM 310). The American bishops have suggested that the priest might *76* lead this ritual at the door of the church before processing to the sanctuary (IOM 74). If so, he should have the vessel nearby or held by a server. If the baptismal font is located near the door, it would be sensible for him to stand there and draw water from it instead of from a separate vessel. *168*

230. The priest invites the people to join him in prayer, asking God to bless the water and to keep them all faithful to the Spirit they have received. The priest may use his own words (RM Appendix 2:2). A brief pause follows to allow time for prayer.

231. The priest joins his hands for the prayer, separating them only to make the sign of the cross over the water at the words of blessing (RM Appendix 2:2). Normally the priest says his prayers with arms outstretched, but this prayer, which incorporates a blessing, calls for his hands to be joined. There are three versions of this prayer in the Missal. The last is designated for the Easter season. In practice, this third version is probably the one used most because Easter is the season when this rite is recommended and most often used. *227*

232. The priest may add salt to the water, but this action is optional (RM Appendix 2:3). In the past, salt was commonly added to holy water to symbolize its exorcistic function. Salt may still be blessed and added where local custom encourages it. In this case the priest asks God to bless the salt, an element used by Elisha (2 Kgs 2:19-22). The prophet alleviated the burden of the people whose water source had gone bad. He prayed that God would make wholesome the water into which he threw salt. God granted the prayer. This little-known episode, which does not appear anywhere in the Lectionary for Mass, is recalled in the prayer over the salt. The priest asks God that the mixture of salt and water might drive out the power of evil and maintain forever the presence of the Holy Spirit. The Missal is not clear about hand gestures, but presumably the priest keeps his hands joined as he did for the previous prayer over the water and makes the sign of the cross during the words of blessing over the salt. After this prayer the priest adds the salt to the water, saying nothing more.

233. The Missal says that the priest sprinkles himself and the ministers, then the clergy and the people. In practice, it would be more dignified for him to dip his fingers in the water and make the sign of the cross over himself rather than take the sprinkler and sprinkle himself. If desired, he may walk throughout the church (RM Appendix 2:4). The Missal does not say how he takes up the sprinkler. It might be resting in a nearby vessel; it might be handed to him by a server. The sequence of sprinkling moves through a hierarchy of ministers. It is not clear if this sequence is meant to designate the hierarchy or to suggest a practical procession from those nearby to those farther away. All the baptized share equally as members of the Body of Christ. There is a distinction between clergy and laity in the church, but a rite recalling baptism seems an inopportune occasion to make this point.

234. The priest may move throughout the church, and the IOM has promoted this suggestion with the option of starting the ritual at the door of the church (74). "So that the rite of sprinkling may clearly point to a renewal of the cleansing waters of Baptism, a sufficient amount of water should be used." For the sake of the sign, it would be preferable if drops of water reached everyone. Depending on the size of the church, this could take some time.

235. The sprinkler may take the traditional form—a metal tube, held by hand, and capped with a perforated lid. The priest dips the sprinkler into the bucket and sprays the water by punching the air. Instead of a metal sprinkler, some priests use a small, freshly pruned, leafy branch or a brush of reeds or straw.

236. In practice, some parishes have invited other ministers to help sprinkle, especially when the assembly is large. After all, everyone may sign themselves with holy water upon entering the church, and the Book of Blessings permits lay ministers to sprinkle objects over which they pray. The GIRM does not address this issue.

237. When catechumens are present, no special instruction is given. But the sprinkling has no meaning as a reminder of baptism for those who have not yet been baptized.

238. During the sprinkling a song may be sung (RM Appendix 2:4). The Missal makes several recommendations, grouped for use during and outside the Easter season. But any appropriate song is permitted. The 2002 RM carried over all seven of the previous texts, including one that

the English sacramentary had never translated, drawn from Daniel 3:77, 79. The 2002 Roman Missal also added a text combined from Wisdom 3:8 and Ezekiel 36:25. Some parishes have sung the *Glory to God* during the sprinkling. It saves time, but that hymn has little to do with this rite. 242

239. When the song is over, the priest at his chair again turns to the people and recites a final text with hands joined. All answer, "Amen" (RM Appendix 2:5). This text presumes that the priest begins the blessing of water at his chair and that the chair might not be facing the people. But there may be occasions when the priest reaches the chair now for the first time (IOM 74), and the chair should be facing the people anyway 234 (GIRM 310). The priest's hands are joined because he speaks of God in 76 the third person to the people, not in direct address. 231

240. In practice, the people's Amen has been weak or non-existent because the priest's final text ends without a clear cue, such as the one that concludes the presidential prayers. Singing the text, though, would supply a good cue.

241. When the blessing and sprinkling of water are used, they replace the entire act of penitence, as well as the *Kyrie*. What follows next is the *Glory to God* (RM Appendix 2:6).

GLORY TO GOD

242. The *Glory to God* is a hymn of praise and petition to God; it is sung or recited on distinctive days of the calendar (OM 8; GIRM 53, 126). It praises God and signals the festivity of the day. The text may not be replaced with a different hymn of praise (GIRM 53) except at Masses with children (DMC 31; IOM 65). Other texts accepted by "competent authority" may facilitate the children's participation, even if these words "do not correspond exactly to the liturgical texts" (DMC 31).

243. The *Glory to God* is used "on Sundays outside the Seasons of Advent and Lent, on solemnities and feasts, and at special celebrations of a more solemn character" (GIRM 53). In some parishes the *Glory to God* has not 153 been recited at all, under the opinion that it may be omitted when it is not sung or that the opening rites of the Mass should be simplified. But the *Glory to God* should be sung or said at all the Masses on the days prescribed. At Masses with children, however, it may be omitted to simplify the opening rites (DMC 40). 226, 373

244. The *Glory to God* appears in the OM as a hymn that is sung or said. The rubric is in the passive voice; that is, it does not indicate who says or sings it. The 2002 OM offers several musical versions of the first few words (8), which the 1975 Missal did not include. Prior to the Second Vatican Council the priest always began the *Glory to God*, and the Missal included several chant versions of the first few words. Whenever the priest sang these words, a choir would usually sing the rest. After the Council the Missal no longer assigned the opening words of the *Glory to God* to the priest, implicitly inviting everyone to begin singing or reciting the text together. There is nothing about the first few words

233 of this hymn that requires an ordained minister to sing them. In practice, though, the old procedure has continued, especially when the *Glory to God* is recited; people get their cue from the priest. The 2002 GIRM officially reverted to the preconciliar practice: "The *Gloria* is intoned by the priest or, if appropriate, by a cantor or by the choir" (53). The 2002 OM supports this preference with its musical phrases for the opening words. The OM does not indicate who sings them, but the notes appear in the book used primarily by the priest. Musical notation for the rest of

379 the text is completely absent from the OM.

245. If the priest is wearing a wireless microphone, shutting it off for the *Glory to God* will ensure that his voice does not overpower that of the faithful.

246. In the chant tradition the phrases of the *Gloria* were often sung in alternation between two choirs or between a cantor and the choir. The GIRM says, "It is sung either by everyone together, or by the people alternately with the choir, or by the choir alone." In recitation, all may speak the text together, or two parts of the congregation may alternate the lines (53). In practice, people usually recite the words together. Some musical versions of the hymn have introduced a refrain sung by all, while the choir sings the rest of the hymn as verses. In 1996 the United States Bishops' Committee on the Liturgy said of this practice, "The addition of refrains to the *Glory to God* is permitted, provided the refrains encourage congregational participation" (*Committee on the Liturgy Newsletter* 33 [January/February 1997] 5). The GIRM does not precisely address this option, but the practice is not far removed from the tradition of alternating the lines of the text. In the interests of the full participation of the faithful, having the choir sing the text alone seems undesirable. The GIRM does

141, 384, not explicitly recommend singing the *Glory to God* in Latin.
622

247. Some parishes sing the *Glory to God* during the Christmas and Easter seasons, omit it during Advent and Lent, and recite it on other Sundays. Others sing it whenever the liturgy calls for it. Still others recite it week after week. It is a hymn; some sung version of it deserves to be in the parish's repertoire.

248. Heads should bow at the name of Jesus in the middle of the text and at the mention of the Trinity at the end (GIRM 275a), but few people observe this.

197

CHANGES TO THE INTRODUCTORY RITES

249. On some occasions the introductory rites are omitted or take on a special character (GIRM 46). For example, there are special ceremonies for Ash Wednesday, Palm Sunday, and the Presentation of the Lord that eliminate the act of penitence. When the baptism of children or the anointing of the sick takes place at a Sunday Mass, the act of penitence is omitted (Rite of Baptism for Children 29; PCS 135–136).

250. In Masses with children some element of the introductory rites may be omitted or expanded, but each should be used from time to time. The introductory rites should always conclude with the collect (DMC 40).

226, 246

COLLECT

251. The collect is the opening prayer of the Mass (OM 9; GIRM 54). Especially on feasts and during seasons it expresses the character of the celebration. The priest invites the people to pray. All observe a brief silence. The priest leads the prayer. All answer, "Amen."

252. The priest and people may sing or speak their parts. Singing is encouraged for texts such as this at Mass (GIRM 40), and the RM supplies chant formulas in the first appendix, but the collect is most frequently spoken in parishes.

141

253. Usually a server holds the Missal for the priest at this time. Some priests like to use the Missal throughout the introductory rites. Others have the words memorized up to this point. But the text of the collect changes at least weekly, and often daily. The GIRM asks the acolyte "to approach the priest . . . in order to present the book" (189), but in parishes a server usually fulfills this role. Many servers step forward on the cue of the spoken words "Let us pray." But the movement of the

199

server, the opening of the book, and the finding of the page can distract the assembly and the ministers from their responsibility to fill the brief silence with prayer. It would help the integrity of the prayer if the server were in place before the priest invited the assembly to pray. The page in the book is ideally marked with a ribbon before Mass begins, so that it may be located without undue distraction.

254. A good presider makes sure he has the people's attention before saying, "Let us pray." After the *Glory to God,* for example, some people clear their throats, set down a hymnal, or shift positions. If the action comes to a halt first, people will be more able to pray. If the priest has shut off a wireless microphone before the *Glory to God,* he turns it on again.

255. The priest is to have his hands joined when he says, "Let us pray" (OM 9; GIRM 54, 127). He may feel that it is more natural to open his hands in a gesture similar to the one used for greeting the people with the words "The Lord be with you" and when he invites them to pray after he has washed his hands. In both instances the words are addressed to the people. The priest should at least maintain eye contact with them. The clasping of the hands probably alerts the assembly to focus their attention on prayer to God. After all, if the sprinkling rite was used, the priest joined his hands while praying the blessing. His joined hands now will contrast with his extended hands during the words of the prayer that follows.

256. There are no instructions for the gestures of the people during this prayer. Many of them bow their heads when they hear "Let us pray." If they fold hands when saying private prayers at home, they might do so at this time to link this communal prayer with their own habits of piety.

257. Some priests expand the words of a text, such as "Let us continue to pray," because the community is already at prayer. But the traditional words are "Let us pray." This simple introduction signals the prayer that immediately follows. It does not imply "Let us pray for the first time." After the Council the Sacramentary had permitted the expansion of this invitation to include words indicating what people should pray for, but the simple formula frees people to pray as they wish.

258. Silence follows (OM 9; GIRM 45, 127) so that everyone "may be conscious of the fact that they are in God's presence and may formulate their petitions mentally" (GIRM 54; IOM 35, 77). Other prayers have already been said, but this one focuses on the needs of this community gathered on this day for this Mass.

259. For this silence to have its effect, it should not be filled by unnecessary movements. The pause serves prayer, not the action of the ministers or the faithful. If priest, server, and people work at this together, the ambient noise of the room will settle, and all will join in communal, silent prayer. *253*

260. The text of the prayer is usually in four parts: an address to God by some title, an acknowledgment of God's mighty deeds, a petition, and a concluding doxology. The prayer is almost always addressed to God through the Son in the Holy Spirit. The GIRM says this prayer sets the character of the celebration (54), but this is truer on feasts and during seasons of the year than during Ordinary Time. The character may be set in the way God is addressed, the deeds for which God is praised, or in the specific petition.

261. On Sundays the text for the opening prayer comes from the Mass of the day, whether it is Easter, the Second Sunday of Advent, or the Thirtieth Sunday in Ordinary Time. There is a wider choice of Masses on most weekdays. At Masses with children the priest may select a differ- *510* ent prayer that better connects with children, preferably from the same liturgical season (DMC 50). He may even adapt the words of the prayer to make them more understandable to children (51).

262. Only one collect is prayed, even though there may be several to choose from (GIRM 54). For example, if the feast of Our Lady of Guadalupe falls on a Sunday in Advent, the collect for Mary is replaced with the one for the season. The pre-Vatican II Missal called for more than one collect on certain days, but that practice is no longer observed in the Roman Rite. *510, 789*

263. The priest extends his hands for the words of the prayer (OM 9; GIRM 127). Prior to the Council a priest used the same gesture for the prayer as he did for the greeting: extending his hands no higher nor wider than his shoulders, palms facing each other. The priest opened and *202, 509,* closed his hands rather quickly for the greeting, but his hands remained *541, 620,* apart for the body of the prayer. Most priests now distinguish these two *788* gestures, choosing for the prayer a gesture traditionally called *orans*, or the praying gesture. The lifting up of hands for prayer is mentioned in Exodus 9:29, 33; Psalms 28:2, 44:20, and 134:2; Isaiah 1:15; and 1 Timothy 2:8. In the early third century Tertullian of North Africa wrote, "Not only do we raise our hands, but we stretch tl m out imitating the suffering of the Lord, and while praying we confes: Christ" (*Prayer* 14). The Council urged a return to the liturgical sources, so many priests have adopted

the wider gesture described by Tertullian and suggested by the Scriptures. Still, there are many variations on how this is done. Some priests lift their arms high, as if reaching toward heaven. Others extend their arms forward or to the side, palms up, as if gathering the faithful. The liturgical documents today do not specify what this gesture looks like, and perhaps this is good. It frees the priest to establish a posture he finds prayerful. He usually joins his hands as his text concludes and the people acclaim, "Amen."

264. The priest is to use a loud and clear voice so that everyone can understand the words of the prayer (GIRM 32). The heart of the prayer is the petition, the third of its four parts. The priest will help the people pray if he especially conveys the meaning of those words. Sometimes a slight pause between them and the concluding doxology is enough to let the purpose of the prayer sink in.

265. When addressing God in prayer, many priests find it helpful to keep their eyes raised to some point near the ceiling at the back of the church, while they refer to the Missal as needed. Others keep their eyes glued to the text in the Missal, but it will usually help the assembly to feel more a part of the prayer if the priest includes them in the space between his face and the place he looks to address God. The IOM wisely cautions the priest not to make eye contact with the assembly when addressing God in prayer (12). He may look above the people, but preferably not at the people. The priest looks at the assembly for statements such as the greeting, but he should look elsewhere for the prayers.

202, 254

266. The presider is to bow his head during the collect at the name of Jesus, the Trinity, and, if applicable, the name of the saint remembered at that Mass (GIRM 275a). Not all observe this, however.

267. The prayer concludes when the priest speaks a Trinitarian formula and all respond "Amen" (OM 9; GIRM 127). The OM says that the people sing or say this word as an acclamation. Too often the faithful mumble the word while eagerly taking their seats. The people should be anxious to affirm the prayer with their Amen. The IOM says they make the prayer their own (35). From the moment the priest says, "Let us pray," through the silence, and into the words of the prayer, the people have been invited to center themselves in the presence of God and to direct their thoughts to heaven. They seal these few moments with their acclamation and draw the introductory rites to a close.

268. All then sit together for the first time (OM 10; GIRM 128). The entrance of latecomers in some churches distracts people from participating in the introductory rites and from listening carefully to the Scriptures. If latecomers need to find seats, this is the ideal time for ushers to assist.   *51*

269. If the priest is wearing a wireless microphone, he should shut it off after the collect.

270. Children may be dismissed for their own Liturgy of the Word after the introductory rites (DMC 17). They may be brought to a separate but not too distant room, in order to hear the Scriptures and a homily appropriate for their level of understanding. They may rejoin the adults for the Liturgy of the Eucharist. Some communities frequently offer this   *407* option to children on Sundays. Others do not, either because they value the presence of the children in the full Eucharistic assembly or because they lack adequate staff or space. The documents do not say who dismisses the children. A deacon gives the dismissal at the end of Mass, so he could appropriately direct the movement of children here. The catechist who will lead the children's Liturgy of the Word might personally invite them. The priest could extend the invitation. Or in communities where this option is regularly featured, no announcement may be necessary at all. Normally, though, someone will deliver a cheerful invitation. Some communities sing a refrain or hear instrumental music as the children leave, but the documents are silent on this practice. Out of respect for those who will give attention to the Scriptures, the departure of the children should be complete before the Liturgy of the Word begins.

Liturgy of the Word

271. The proclamation of the Scriptures brings the community into the presence of the living God who speaks to them here and now. It is not a mere reading of old texts. "When the Sacred Scriptures are read in the Church, God himself speaks to his people, and Christ, present in his own word, proclaims the Gospel" (GIRM 29). Christ is present above all in the Eucharist, but Christ is also present in the Scriptures (LM 46). It is not the priest or deacon who proclaims the gospel. It is Christ who proclaims the gospel. The people hear his words through the medium of the minister's voice.

272. The Liturgy of the Word includes the readings from Scripture, the responsory, the gospel acclamation, the homily, the profession of faith, and the prayer of the faithful. In the Scriptures God speaks to the people. In silence and singing, the people make God's word their own. In the Creed they affirm their adherence to God's word. In the prayer of the faithful those who have been nourished by God's word pray for the needs of the Church and the world (GIRM 55).

CHOICE OF READINGS

273. The Lectionary arranges the biblical readings for the Masses of the year (GIRM 57, 362). Options are available on certain days of the year, such as Christmas and the Pentecost Vigil, and for certain occasions, such as weddings and devotional Masses (LM 78–91). The presider makes use of these options "in harmony with all concerned and after listening to the opinions of the faithful in what concerns them" (40).

274. At Masses with children, if the readings of the day seem unsuited for them, "it is permissible to choose readings or a reading either from the Lectionary of the Roman Missal or directly from the Bible" (DMC 43). Paraphrases, though, should be avoided (45).

275. At children's Masses, if the participants would be unable to comprehend the various Scripture readings, "it is permissible to read two

or only one of them," even on Sundays, "but the reading of the gospel should never be omitted" (DMC 42). On Palm Sunday the first and/or second readings may be omitted at any Mass if "pastoral reasons suggest" (LM 38ABC).

366

276. The Scriptures may not be replaced with non-biblical texts (GIRM 57).

INTRODUCTION TO THE LITURGY OF THE WORD

277. The priest may give an introduction to the Liturgy of the Word (GIRM 31, 128). The deacon may give introductions at Mass (171d), presumably including this one. The LM explicitly permits the deacon or someone else—a commentator, for example—to read this introduction (42). *293, 298*

278. The one who presides at the Liturgy of the Word usually composes these comments and preaches the homily (LM 38), but these tasks may be shared. The comments should help people understand what they *359* will hear and "stir up an attitude of faith and good will" (42). The words should be "concise . . . simple, faithful to the text, brief, well prepared, and properly varied to suit the text they introduce" (15). They work best before the first reading. If they are given before the other readings, they could intrude on the spirit of the Liturgy of the Word.

279. This introduction may also be given at Masses with children. When the children celebrate Mass on a saint's day, for example, an excerpt from the life of that saint or an explanation of the readings may be given at the start of the Liturgy of the Word (DMC 47).

280. As with all commentary, a little goes a long way. An introduction to the Scriptures may dull the senses of the faithful more than it helps them listen. Most parishes omit this option.

281. Alternatively, all may observe a brief period of silence before the Liturgy of the Word begins (LM 28). In silence, all would pray for God to open their minds and hearts to the word. But if the community is unaccustomed to silence here, it will feel uncomfortable, as if the lector has missed a cue. If silence is desired, the lector might advance to the ambo and pause for silent prayer before stepping into it. At a minimum, the lector will want to have the attention of all before proclaiming the first reading.

LECTOR

282. The GIRM assumes that the normal lector is a man instituted for this role in a liturgical ceremony conducted by a bishop (99), although it allows other laypersons commissioned to proclaim the readings in the absence of an instituted lector (101). The duties of a lector are enumerated in 194–198, and RS 44 states that those paragraphs refer to the commissioned layperson, not to the instituted lector. But the GIRM indicates otherwise (99). The LM requested the service of instituted lectors "at least on Sundays and festive days, especially at the principal Mass of the day," when such lectors are available (51). Instituted lectors may prepare "others of the faithful who may be appointed on a given occasion to read at Mass" (LM 51). They may assist in the "arrangement of the Liturgy of the Word," although it is not clear what that means. Perhaps it refers to opening the Lectionaries to the right page and appointing ministers for proclamation. In the absence of musicians, the lector may read the entrance and Communion antiphons (GIRM 48, 198).

283. Nonetheless, the duties of an instituted lector may be carried out by a commissioned layperson, even by children (DMC 47). "The liturgical assembly truly requires readers, even those not instituted" (LM 52). They should be trained with spiritual, biblical, and liturgical formation, as well as the technical preparation for reading publicly (52, 55). At almost every Catholic parish Sunday Mass, non-instituted lectors, both male and female, proclaim the readings. It would seem uncharitable to have the bishop institute the males but not the females of a given parish into the ministry of lector. So almost all parish lectors are commissioned, not instituted.

284. In the absence of any lector, a deacon may proclaim the first readings (GIRM 171f., 176; LM 49). In the absence of lectors and a deacon, the priest may read all the Scriptures (GIRM 59, 135; LM 49), but this is not ideal (GIRM 91). The proclamation of the Scriptures belongs to ministers other than the presider. Even if concelebrants and deacons are present, lectors proclaim the first readings (LM 51).

285. If there is more than one reading, it is preferable to use a different lector for each (GIRM 109; LM 52). However, the 2002 GIRM says it is not appropriate for one reading to be proclaimed by two lectors, one after the other, except for the proclamation of the Passion on Palm Sunday and Good Friday (109). This ruling surprised people in parishes where the use of multiple readers had enhanced the proclamation of long narrative gospels such as those of the woman at the well, the man born blind, and

the raising of Lazarus (Sundays 3, 4 and 5 of Lent, Year A). The GIRM does not explain why this custom is appropriate for the Passion but not for other passages.

286. At children's Masses more than one lector may share the same reading (LMC 52). "When the text of the readings lends itself to this, it may be helpful to have the children read it with parts distributed among them, as is provided for the reading of the Lord's passion during Holy Week" (DMC 47).

287. At some multilingual Masses, different readers proclaim the same reading more than one time in various languages. The GIRM does not specifically address this situation, but it is generally inadvisable to repeat parts of the Mass. At papal Masses it is common to hear each reading proclaimed once, each in a different language. Some parishes do the same, printing participation aids with the readings in a language different from the one in which each is proclaimed. This solution allows a greater number to appreciate the meaning of the Scriptures, but it relies on economic resources for printing and compromises the ideal of having the faithful hear the Scriptures in the liturgy rather than read them.

288. Lectors generally wear "ordinary attire," "in keeping with the customs of the different regions" (LM 54). An instituted lector wears an alb *93* as well as an amice and cincture if needed (GIRM 336; LM 54). Lectors in the United States "may wear the alb or other suitable vesture or other appropriate and dignified clothing" (GIRM 339; IOM 57).

APPROACHING THE AMBO

289. The lector usually sits in the assembly with other worshipers. The GIRM indicates that a vested lector sits in the sanctuary (195), but this refers to an instituted lector. In some parishes the non-instituted lector sits in the sanctuary at least through the Liturgy of the Word. But in most parish churches the lector sits in ordinary attire with the assembly. *189*

290. The readings are proclaimed at the ambo (OM 10; GIRM 58, 196, 309; LM 16). To approach the ambo (GIRM 128), the lector leaves his or *73* her place and enters the sanctuary. It would be proper for the lector to make a profound bow to the altar before entering the sanctuary (CB 72). If the lector is already seated in the sanctuary near the ambo, no reverence to the altar is needed.

291. The lector can minimize distractions if the Lectionary has been opened to the proper page prior to Mass. On occasion, though, upon reaching the ambo, the lector may need to open the Lectioʃ·ʃy, turn a page, or move a ribbon. This should take place before announcing the reading. This physical preparation on the part of the lector can help the assembly prepare itself physically and spiritually for the word of God.

PROCLAIMING THE READINGS

292. The Lectionary usually rests on top of the ambo while the lector reads. Some lectors pick up and hold the book. A lot depends on the height of the ambo, the location of the microphone, the weight of the book, and the ability of the lector to read the text and maintain eye contact with the assembly. The ambo may be constructed in a way that the lector need not lift the book. If the lectors of a parish lift the book to see the words more plainly, they should be careful not to obscure the view of the faithful nor to place the Lectionary between their mouth and the microphone. The liturgical documents say nothing about the lector holding the book.

293. At the head of each reading the Lectionary presents the exact citation of biblical verses together with a one-sentence summary. Traditionally the lector does not read these aloud. If a minister gives an introduction to one or more of the readings, the summary might serve as an aid. The lector does read aloud the announcement that precedes the reading; for example, "A reading from the Book of Exodus." Due to the ritual nature of this statement, it is best not to vary it with redundancies such as "Today's first reading is a reading from the Book of Exodus."

294. Throughout the readings lectors should speak with strong, clear voices, signaling their understanding of the text (LM 14; IOM 10, 14). Good lectors establish eye contact with the faithful as much as possible and adjust the pace and volume of the proclamation to the acoustics of the church. If the lector makes a mistake that needs to be corrected, it is usually best to back up a phrase and read it again without interjecting extra words such as "Excuse me." If some accidental noise overpowers the room—feedback in the sound system, jet engines overhead, a crash in the sacristy—the lector may pause if necessary and resume speaking when the noise clears. The less attention drawn to mishaps the more people can focus on the word of God.

295. At the conclusion of the reading, the lector should observe silence with everyone else. Sometimes the lector turns the page for the next reading or

removes the Lectionary to make room for the gospel book. Although these actions are polite, they can distract from the silence that everyone should be observing. The silence is for prayer, not for shuffling paper. In some parishes the lector returns to his or her place immediately after the reading and observes silence from there, but even this movement can break the effect. After the people's acclamation the lector might take a step back, lower his or her head, and stand at rest. The documents do not assert a preference. Whatever the lector does, it should look natural and prayerful.

296.   The lector may sing the reading (GIRM 40; LM 14). Styles may vary   *141* according to cultures. The first appendix of the RM suggests a variety of tones to which the readings may be chanted. This is rarely done at parish Masses.

HEARING THE READINGS

297.   While the lector reads, everyone else sits (GIRM 43) and listens (OM 10; GIRM 128, 130). Because it is God's own word in the readings and Christ who speaks in the gospel, "all must listen with reverence" (GIRM 29). Inward and outward reverence "will bring them continuous growth in the spiritual life and draw them more deeply into the mystery which is celebrated" (LM 45).

298.   Some churches provide the assembly with a copy of the texts the lector reads. Many argue that this helps the faithful hear. However, the ideal expressed in the liturgical documents is that one person reads and everyone else listens. If the faithful need additional help to follow the readings, an introduction may be given, or people may be encouraged to pray over the Scriptures at home before coming to church. People will   *38, 277* usually feel more present to the proclamation if all turn their attention to the reader instead of participation aids.

CONCLUDING THE READINGS

299.   At the conclusion the lector announces, "The word of the Lord," and all respond, "Thanks be to God" (OM 10; GIRM 59, 128). A good lector pauses just before making this announcement to let the text of the reading settle in the ears of the listeners.

300.   The GIRM encourages the singing of this acclamation (40), and the first appendix of the RM offers notes for chanting. The LM allows this to be sung by someone other than the lector (18), but GIRM 59 says,

". . . whoever reads gives the acclamation," and 128 agrees. However, at papal Masses a cantor sometimes sings the acclamation after the lector has finished the reading.

301. Some lectors lift the book while announcing, "The word of the Lord." There is no such rubric, and the gesture draws unnecessary attention to the book. The word of the Lord is the sound that was proclaimed, not the book that helped make it. God speaks through the proclamation, and the people are acclaiming what they have heard.

302. Some lectors still say, "This is the word of the Lord," the formula first in use after the Council. The correct formula omits the first two words and better draws attention to the proclamation. It resembles the formulas
728, 733 used at Communion: "The Body of Christ" and "The Blood of Christ."

FIRST READING

303. The Liturgy of the Word opens with a reading (OM 10; GIRM 128). Once at the ambo, the lector for the first reading should wait until everyone is seated and settled before beginning. People will need a few moments to find their places, move belongings, and give attention to children. Even though their sitting is only a change in posture, it represents a break for members of the assembly, who may be exchanging some words or acknowledging one another's presence in this brief moment. A good lector will let this happen and give people a chance to focus their
281, 317 attention on the reading.

304. Silence follows the first reading, while all meditate on what they have heard (GIRM 45, 56, 128; LM 28). It will probably help if the lec-
295, 317 tor remains at the ambo during this silence. The lector may return to his or her place when the psalm begins, unless the lector also serves as the psalmist of that Mass. If the lector goes into the nave at this time, it would be appropriate for him or her to make a profound bow to the altar upon leaving the sanctuary (CB 72). If the lector is to proclaim the second reading, he or she may need to step aside for the psalmist to use the ambo. But the lector may remain in the sanctuary during the psalm, face the psalmist, and join the assembly in the response.

RESPONSORIAL PSALM

305. The responsorial psalm follows the first reading (OM 11). It "fosters meditation on the word of God" (GIRM 61). On some occasions the

responsory is a canticle from the Old or New Testament, not precisely a psalm. Canticles and psalms have the same form, but those found in the Book of Psalms are called psalms.

306. The GIRM refers to the psalmist as a role distinct from that of the cantor and the lector (61, 99, 102, 129, 196, 352), but in the absence of a psalmist, a cantor or lector may lead the psalm. The documents never mention a choir singing the psalm. This may be an oversight, or it may have to do with the preference that the psalm be led from the ambo (GIRM 309; LM 22), since the choir sings from another place (GIRM 312). However, *310* the ambo should be large enough to accommodate several ministers at the same time (LM 34). In practice, some choirs assist on verses of the psalm, and the scriptural texts of the psalm sometimes presume that several voices are singing. The gradual, which may substitute for the psalm, requires the assistance of a choir (*Ordo Cantus Missae* 5). The en- *311* tire assembly would logically assume the role of the psalmist when the responsory is sung in metrical forms (GIRM 61). Normally, though, the GIRM has a psalmist in mind. The psalmist should sing skillfully (GIRM 102), but so should the cantor. The ideal separation of the role shows the distinct ministry of the one who leads the psalm, which is integral to the proclamation of the Scriptures in the Liturgy of the Word. *58*

307. It is preferable that the psalm be sung (OM 11; GIRM 61; LM 20, 21). The one who leads the psalm should have the skills of singing and enunciating (GIRM 102; LM 56), prayerfully entering the spirit of the psalm and leading the assembly's worship.

308. The psalmist breaks the silence that follows the first reading (cf. GIRM 128). If the psalm is sung, the instrument that accompanies it *304* may break the silence with its introduction. Or the psalmist disrupts the stillness of the room by moving to the ambo while the lector steps aside. In practice, then, if the psalm is sung, someone in the music ministry determines the length of the silence that follows the first reading. The length of this pause will vary from parish to parish. Some find fifteen seconds long enough; others take thirty seconds or more.

309. The assigned psalm usually coheres with the first reading. Brief remarks may be made to explain the psalm before it is sung (LM 19). Someone (the LM does not say who—the priest, the deacon, the commentator, the lector, the psalmist, or the cantor) could give this introduction, but probably not from the ambo (cf. GIRM 105b; LM 33). Most parishes have

decided against having an introduction to the psalm because it intrudes on the flow of the Liturgy of the Word and threatens to clutter the early part of the Mass with too many commentaries. Many communities avoid announcing the psalm at all, relying on a hymn board or participation aid to help people find the text and music. By avoiding an announcement before the psalm, it is treated more like the other readings, and the Liturgy of the Word unfolds more prayerfully.

205, 277

310. The psalm is to be led from the ambo (GIRM 309; LM 22), but "another suitable place" is acceptable (GIRM 61). In some churches the distance between the ambo and the choir is great, or the sanctuary is not easily accessible. In such circumstances the cantor may sing the psalm apart from the ambo, wherever the musicians lead. If the psalmist enters the sanctuary from some other place, it would be appropriate for him or her to make a profound bow to the altar (CB 72).

311. To start, the psalmist usually sings a refrain that the people repeat. Then the psalmist sings the verses, alternating with the people's refrain (GIRM 129, 196). Throughout the Easter season and on some other days, the Lectionary permits the entire antiphon to be replaced with an Alleluia. Instead of this format, the psalm may be sung straight through without a response, even in metrical form such as a hymn. If a congregation finds it hard to sing a new psalm every week, the psalm of the day may be replaced with one from the appropriate common psalms in the Lectionary. Or the psalmist may sing the verses assigned for the day, while everyone else sings a better known refrain from the common responses in the Lectionary. Other songs and hymns should not replace the psalm (GIRM 61; LM 89). The gradual from the Roman Gradual may replace the psalm (GIRM 61), but this is rarely done. The gradual is an antiphon started by a cantor and completed by a choir, which continues to sing the verse with or without repeating the antiphon. The antiphon to the gradual need not be repeated after its verse. A simple gradual may be started by a cantor or choir and taken up by the assembly. It has several verses, and the antiphon is repeated after each one. Either kind of gradual is rarely sung because there are so few musical versions. Non-biblical texts may not be substituted for the responsorial psalm (GIRM 57).

312. After the psalm, if the psalmist needs to move from the ambo to another area of the church, it would be appropriate for him or her to make a profound bow to the altar when leaving the sanctuary (CB 72).

313. The psalm may be recited (GIRM 61), though this is not preferred. If the lector also leads the psalm, he or she should allow silence after the first reading before proceeding (GIRM 128). If people do not have the text of the antiphon in some participation aid, the leader of the psalm should help them, especially after the first verse.

314. When there is only one reading before the gospel, the psalm is not to be omitted (GIRM 63a, b). The pre-2002 GIRM permitted leaving out the psalm if the gospel acclamation was to be sung (38b), but this omission was rarely done. Nonetheless, at children's Masses the singing of the psalm may be replaced with silence (DMC 46).

315. If incense will be used at the gospel, this would be a good time for the thurifer to retrieve the thurible and the boat from the stand and be prepared to bring them to the priest during the gospel acclamation.   *333*

SECOND READING

316. After the psalm a reading from the New Testament may be proclaimed (OM 12; GIRM 128). At some Masses there is no second reading before the gospel.

317. No silence needs to follow the responsorial psalm (LM 28). After the psalm the lector approaches the ambo (OM 12). If the lector enters the sanctuary at this time, he or she would appropriately bow to the altar (CB 72). All listen to the reading, respond with the acclamation, and observe silence afterward (GIRM 130).   *303, 304*

318. At the conclusion of the second reading, silence is observed. Many ambos are too small to accommodate both the Lectionary and the Book of the Gospels. A helpful lector will move the Lectionary aside to make room. Some have a shelf where the lector places the Lectionary. In other churches the lector or a server removes the Lectionary to the credence table or the sacristy. If all this movement is reserved until the gospel acclamation begins, it will not disturb the silence after the reading.   *295*

319. If the lector has waited at the ambo throughout the silence, he or she moves the Lectionary aside and returns to his or her place once the music for the gospel acclamation begins. In most churches the lector's place is outside the sanctuary; therefore, it would be appropriate for the lector to make a profound bow to the altar upon leaving the sanctuary (CB 72).

SEQUENCE

320. The sequence, taken from the Lectionary, is a liturgical hymn that relates to a particular feast or season. The only occasions when the sequence is obligatory are Easter Sunday and Pentecost (GIRM 64). It is sung after the second reading, before the gospel acclamation. The pre-2000 GIRM did not explicitly say when the sequence was to be sung (40), but it mentioned this hymn after its treatment of the gospel acclamation. When the revised GIRM was first published in 2000, it said the sequence should be sung *after* the Alleluia (64), in agreement with the *Ordo Cantus Missae* in the *Graduale Romanum* (8). But the 2002 GIRM changed the order to what had already become a more common practice: the sequence is to come *before* the Alleluia.

321. The GIRM does not say what the posture of the assembly should be during the sequence (43). If all are singing the sequence, it would make sense for all to stand. But if a distinction between the sequence and the gospel seems important, all could remain seated.

322. The *Ordo Cantus Missae* says if the Alleluia and its verse are not sung, the sequence is omitted (8). But on Easter and Pentecost, the only two days the sequence is obligatory, it is hoped that at least the Alleluia and its verse would be sung. In practice, many parishes sing a metrical version of the sequence to a familiar hymn tune. Others recite the text together or in alternation. Still others omit it altogether, but on Easter and Pentecost the sequence should be said or sung.

GOSPEL ACCLAMATION

323. The gospel acclamation follows the second reading (OM 13; GIRM 131). With this text "the assembly of the faithful welcomes and greets the Lord who is about to speak to it in the gospel and professes its faith by means of the chant" (GIRM 62; cf. LM 23).

324. Usually a cantor sings the acclamation once, and then all repeat it. If the acclamation is lengthy or well known, all may sing it together the first time. The cantor then sings the verse, and all repeat the acclamation. In place of the cantor, a choir may lead the acclamation and sing the verse. Throughout most of the year, the acclamation is "Alleluia," but during Lent an alternative text is used (GIRM 62).

325. The verse is usually taken from the Lectionary. It may be drawn from the Roman Gradual instead (GIRM 62), but the Lectionary is more accessible.

326. During Lent the tract may be sung in place of the gospel acclamation (GIRM 62), but this is rarely done. The tract is a series of psalm verses sung alternately by divisions of singers. Texts and chants for the tract are in the *Graduale Romanum*.

327. The gospel acclamation breaks the silence that follows the second reading (GIRM 45, 130; LM 28). Whoever leads the acclamation should allow sufficient time for silence.

328. The psalmist may also lead the gospel acclamation (LM 56; IOM 18). But another cantor or the choir may lead it instead.

329. The gospel acclamation is not led from the ambo (GIRM 309; LM 33). The cantor usually leads the acclamation from a cantor's stand or someplace in the music area.

330. The gospel acclamation may be omitted if it is not sung (GIRM 63c), but this refers to Masses with one reading before the gospel, not to Sunday Mass. On Sundays the gospel acclamation "is sung" (62a, b). The LM says more strongly, "The *Alleluia* or the verse before the Gospel must be sung, and during it all stand. It is not to be sung only by the cantor who intones it or by the choir, but by the whole of the people together" (23). Singing the gospel acclamation is quite common in parishes, especially on Sundays, but on weekdays it is often omitted. Those who recite the gospel acclamation quickly discover they have diminished its usefulness as a greeting to the Lord.

331. The gospel acclamation may be another good time for ushers to seat latecomers. It is best if people are not trying to find seats in the assembly during the proclamation of the Scriptures.   51

ACTIONS DURING THE GOSPEL ACCLAMATION

332. As the acclamation begins, all stand (GIRM 43, 131). The assembly's posture and song show honor to the Book of the Gospels (LM 17).

333. If incense is used, it is prepared at this time (OM 14; GIRM 276c). Usually the thurifer or deacon or both assist (GIRM 175). They bring the thurible to the priest, who spoons incense from the boat onto the burning

coals and blesses the smoke silently by making the sign of the cross with his hand (132).

334. The gospel is to be proclaimed by a deacon or, in his absence, by a priest (GIRM 59; LM 49). Ideally, the presider does not proclaim any of the readings. By tradition, that responsibility falls to other ministers. If a deacon or another priest is not present, however, the presider will process to the ambo and read the gospel.

335. If there is a deacon, he presents himself to the priest and makes a profound bow to him while asking quietly for the blessing (OM 14; GIRM 175, 275b; LM 17). The priest gives the blessing quietly while making the sign of the cross over the deacon. New to the 2002 GIRM, the deacon makes the sign of the cross over himself. He answers, "Amen." The GIRM is not clear about when the deacon straightens up. His bow is to accompany the request, so presumably he stands up straight for the blessing, though many deacons bow through it.

PROCESSION

336. The minister who proclaims the gospel goes to the ambo in procession (OM 14–15). In a way this movement is no different from that of a lector walking up to the ambo, but because of the significance of the gospel, several things do and may happen to set this procession apart.

337. Ministers may carry the thurible and lighted candles and lead the procession to the ambo (GIRM 133, 175). The GIRM first mentions the ministers after the deacon or priest has grasped the Book of the Gospels, but logically they will precede him to the altar, and from the altar to the ambo. Traditionally the thurifer leads and two candle bearers follow. The IOM lists this procession among the responsibilities of altar servers (22). In addition to incense and candles, ministers may carry "other symbols of reverence that may be customary" (LM 17). It is not clear what these are—perhaps banners or insignia. Children may join this procession (DMC 34). Their participation "makes clear the presence of Christ announcing the word to his people." The IOM says "ushers may assist . . . with processions" (23).

338. If there is no deacon, the priest joins his hands, makes a profound bow toward the altar, and prays quietly to be made worthy to proclaim the gospel (OM 14; GIRM 132, 275b). This is the first of several prayers the priest prays in his own name, "asking that he may exercise his ministry

with greater attention and devotion" (GIRM 33). The documents say that he makes this prayer before the altar. Some priests do this at the chair. But especially if the chair is to the side of the altar, other priests walk to the altar and bow there. In the latter case the procession begins before he says his quiet prayer.

339. If a deacon is to proclaim the gospel, he walks from the priest's chair, where he has just received a blessing, to the altar, where he makes a profound bow (GIRM 175). *335*

340. The priest or deacon then picks up the Book of the Gospels and carries it slightly elevated in procession to the ambo (GIRM 133, 175; LM 17). If the book has been resting on a stand, this would be an appropriate time for a server to remove it from the altar to the credence table. *177* Normally the procession takes the shortest path to the ambo, but for special events some ministers take a longer route. If they do, it should look festive, not as though they have lost their way. If the thurifer and candle bearers are present, they lead the way and arrange themselves around the deacon or priest (OM 15). The thurifer should stand within easy reach of the deacon or priest. The candle bearers traditionally stand on either side of the ambo without obstructing the view of the people.

341. If there is no deacon and no lector, the priest proclaims all the readings (GIRM 135). To process with the Book of the Gospels, he would have to go from the ambo to the altar and back again. If incense is used, he places some in the thurible while standing at the ambo. This solution ignores the diversity of ministries and minimizes the solemnity of the gospel. *284, 333, 334*

342. As the procession reaches the ambo, everyone turns toward the ambo "as a sign of special reverence to the Gospel of Christ" (GIRM 133). This rubric is unnecessary in most churches, where the ambo is in the sanctuary, plainly visible from the nave. Most people naturally face the ambo whether they sit or stand. In some older churches, however, especially those built before the invention of electrical sound reinforcement, the ambo is along the side wall. If for any reason people have not been seeing the ambo from their seats, they should stand and face that direction as a sign of reverence for the gospel.

GOSPEL

343. "The reading of the Gospel is the high point of the Liturgy of the Word" (GIRM 60; LM 13). All the Scriptures are the Word of God, but *271* "Christ, present in his own word, proclaims the Gospel" (GIRM 29).

344. "At the ambo the priest opens the book" (GIRM 134). Logically, a deacon would do the same. This action should not attract attention. It precedes the greeting of the people. If the minister is turning pages while addressing the people, his words will seem insincere.

345. The deacon or priest addresses the people with the traditional greeting, "The Lord be with you" (OM 15). He says these words with hands joined (GIRM 134, 175). The people respond. The greeting and response mutually bestow a gift of faith in the presence of Christ, whose words are about to be heard. The 2002 GIRM specified that the deacon or priest makes the greeting with hands joined, not extended. This rubric, which existed in the pre-Vatican II Missal, was omitted after the Council. In the past the priest said this greeting and then read the gospel with his back to the people. People would not have seen the priest's hands if he had extended them for the greeting. After the Council many priests and deacons, facing the people for the gospel, extended their hands toward the people they were addressing, as they do at the other greetings of the Mass. Now hands are to be joined, as they are when the deacon or priest invites all to offer a sign of peace and when he dismisses the assembly. The GIRM does not explain why. This change back to the former tradition may imply a division of roles: the deacon greets the people with the same words the priest uses, but his role is different. Even a priest who proclaims the gospel is not exercising his presidential role when he greets the people before reading; the proclamation of the Scriptures belongs to other ministers. Still, it has been common to see a deacon or priest extend hands toward the people at this time. The gesture seems to fit the words. Some people in the assembly extend their hands back to the deacon or priest when they make their response. There is no such rubric, but many feel that the mutual gestures make the words more expressive and prepare everyone to hear the gospel.

200, 802

635, 814

284, 341

203

346. This greeting and its response may be sung to bring out the importance of the gospel and to stir up the faith of those who hear it (LM 17). Sample chants are given in the first appendix of the Missal, but these are rarely sung.

347. The deacon or priest announces the gospel to be read: "A reading from the holy Gospel according to N." He uses his thumb to sign a cross upon the book, his own forehead, mouth, and breast (OM 15; GIRM 134, 175; LM 17). All present answer, "Glory to you, Lord." Meanwhile, they sign themselves with their thumb on the forehead, mouth, and breast

(GIRM 134). It has long been traditional for the entire assembly to make this gesture, but it appeared in the GIRM for the first time in 2002. The new sentence seems to say that the people also make the sign of the cross on the book, but this has not been the tradition, nor is it practical.

348.   If incense is used, the deacon or priest about to read the gospel takes the thurible, makes a profound bow to the book, swings the thurible three times toward the book, bows again, and hands the thurible back to the thurifer (OM 15; GIRM 134, 175, 276c, 277). Traditionally the thurifer remains near the ambo while the gospel is proclaimed, letting the thurible gently sway and diffuse its smoke.

349.   The deacon or priest proclaims the gospel. This is the high point of the Liturgy of the Word (GIRM 60).

350.   The deacon or priest signals the end of the gospel with a spoken formula, and the people respond with praise to Christ (OM 16; GIRM 134, 175). The singing of such acclamations is encouraged (GIRM 40; LM 17) but rarely practiced. The first appendix of the Missal gives sample chants.   *141*

351.   The deacon or priest then kisses the book and prays quietly that the words of the gospel may wipe everyone's sins away (OM 16; GIRM 134, 175; LM 17). This text is one of many praying for forgiveness of sins   *164* throughout the Mass. It is one of the private prayers recited for the benefit   *221* of the minister (GIRM 33), and not to be proclaimed aloud as if it were a presidential prayer, even though its content involves the assembly. If kissing the book does not harmonize with the culture of some region,   *338* the Apostolic See may approve another sign established by that local conference of bishops (GIRM 273).

352.   All are seated after the gospel (GIRM 43). The OM, usually careful about rubrics governing the posture of the assembly, omits this instruction.

353.   The Book of the Gospels may remain on the ambo. Some parishes have a shelf or stand for the Book of the Gospels in, on, or near the ambo. BLS says, "It has become customary"—though the practice is not widespread—"to provide a place for the permanent display of the Scriptures in the sanctuary area. This can be done using the front of the ambo or another kind of pedestal" (fn. 84). The English translation of the GIRM says the deacon may remove the Book of the Gospels to the credence table or some other appropriate and dignified place (175), but the Latin original does not mention the deacon. Any minister may do this. The

GIRM does not say where the thurifer and candle bearers go after the gospel, but traditionally they move back to their places. It would not be appropriate to simulate another procession of the gospel book.

354. If much time will elapse between the gospel and the preparation of the gifts, and if incense is being used, the thurifer, sacristan, or another minister may need to add more charcoal to the thurible.

355. If a deacon has proclaimed the gospel, he is to return "to the priest's side" (GIRM 175), but if the priest is going to preach at the ambo, he may be moving at this time. More precisely, the deacon returns to his chair. If the deacon or the priest passes the altar, he makes a profound bow to it (CB 72).

HOMILY

356. The homily is a talk delivered by the priest or deacon to explain the sacred mysteries and to inspire fidelity to the Christian way of life (OM 17; GIRM 65, 136; LM 41). "Through the course of the liturgical year the homily sets forth the mysteries of faith and the standards of the Christian life on the basis of the sacred text" (LM 24). It may also treat another text from the ordinary or proper of the Mass of the day, taking into account the feast or season and the needs of the listeners (GIRM 65).

357. The homily is so integral to the Liturgy of the Word that it may not be omitted on Sundays or holy days without a serious reason. It is recommended on other days (OM 17), especially on weekdays of Advent, Lent, and Easter; whenever people gather in numbers (GIRM 66); and in Masses with children and special groups (LM 25). In parishes it is common to hear a homily every day of the year.

358. Churchgoers sometimes complain about the length of homilies. The Liturgy of the Word and the Liturgy of the Eucharist should be balanced enough to proclaim the mystery of Christ together. The homily will not seem long if it is well prepared and delivered, conceived as part of the whole of the liturgy. It should be "truly the fruit of meditation, carefully prepared, neither too long nor too short, and suited to all those present, even children and the uneducated" (LM 24).

359. By definition, a homily is the talk given by a priest or deacon (OM 17). It is ordinarily delivered by the priest who celebrates the Mass (GIRM 66; LM 24). The celebrant may ask the deacon to preach the homily (GIRM

66, 171c). The priest may never entrust it to a layperson (GIRM 66). At Masses with children, "With the consent of the pastor or rector of the church, one of the adults may speak to the children after the gospel, especially if the priest finds it difficult to adapt himself to the mentality of children. In this matter the norms soon to be issued by the Congregation for the Clergy should be observed" (DMC 24). Those norms permit bishops to delegate laypersons to preach when the celebrant is unable or on special occasions when laypersons "have special qualifications" and their words "are likely to be especially effective" (Letter of Cardinal J. Wright, Prot. 144823/1, 20 November 1973; cf. 2, 4). The IOM says, "Such preaching has its own importance, though it is not a homily" (94).

360. In practice, some pastors have invited laypersons to speak during homily time about diocesan or parochial financial appeals. Religious and other lay missionaries have explained their work and sought support. RS says that instruction or testimony by a layperson should follow the prayer after Communion. Such talks should not "be confused with the homily, nor is it permissible to dispense with the homily on their account" (74). Cardinal Wright's letter had proposed a different solution: "If circumstances permit, the celebrant gives an introduction or conclusion to sermons by the laity" (3).

796

361. The priest delivers his homily standing at the chair, the ambo, or "in another suitable place" (GIRM 136). Some priests like to walk around while they preach. A bishop sits in his chair to preach, but he too may choose another place to be more easily seen and heard (CB 142). The IOM overlooks this option: "the priest celebrant gives the homily while standing at the ambo or at his chair" (94), the same locations given in the LM (26), which predates the GIRM. The GIRM's sequence of optional locations lists the chair first, giving it some preference. If a deacon has proclaimed the gospel, the presider need not go to the ambo to preach. If the priest has proclaimed the gospel, he has the option of returning to the chair for the homily. If he is wearing a wireless microphone and preaching where there is no other microphone, he switches it on.

73, 75

362. The GIRM does not say where a deacon stands if he preaches. Presumably he has the same options the priest does, but the deacon's chair does not hold the same liturgical weight as the presider's. Better options for the deacon are the ambo or another suitable place.

363. When children are present, the homily may take different forms. If they are in the minority, the preacher may address them at some point in

his talk (DMC 17), but this can break its unity. If the number of children is large, the entire homily may be directed to them (19). Children's art may illustrate the homily (36). The preacher may engage these young people in dialogue (48).

364. A good preacher will wait until everyone is seated and settled before beginning to speak. He will avoid beginning and ending the talk with the sign of the cross (IOM 94), a gesture and text that belongs at the beginning of the Mass and during blessings. Some preachers have made parish announcements at the beginning or end of the homily. This practice suggests that the presider never has anyone's attention unless the people are seated. It moves announcements to the most populated part of the Mass—latecomers having arrived and early leavers still in the pew. But it places a higher value on the numbers present than on the integrity of the homily and the concluding rites of the Mass. "Any necessary announcements are to be kept completely separate from the homily; they must take place following the prayer after Communion" (LM 27).

191, 807

795

365. After the homily the preacher sits down. If he passes the altar while going to his chair, he makes a profound bow to the altar (CB 72). It is appropriate for all to observe some moments of silence to reflect on what they have heard (GIRM 45, 56, 136; LM 28).

366. A song may follow the homily at children's Masses in which only one reading was proclaimed (DMC 46). In such instances that reading should have been the gospel. If the psalm and gospel acclamation were omitted, it would be appropriate to sing something after the homily.

275

367. If the priest is wearing a wireless microphone and if he did not need it for preaching, he switches it on before leading the next rites at the chair.

DISMISSAL OF CATECHUMENS

368. Catechumens may be kindly dismissed after the homily (RCIA 67; 83.2). The RCIA gives sample formulas for the priest. This may be an oversight: this dismissal was traditionally given by the deacon.

369. When the priest and deacon stand to announce the dismissal, the people will probably stand as well. The documents give no instruction for the posture of the faithful for the dismissal, but it would be polite for all to stand even though only some are being addressed.

370. The RCIA recommends texts for minor exorcisms (94) and blessings (97). These are envisioned first for celebrations held especially for the catechumens, but they also apply to participation in the Liturgy of the Word at the Sunday Mass (81). If an exorcism is prayed, the catechumens bow or kneel while the celebrant stands with hands outstretched. If a blessing is prayed, catechumens stand for the prayer and then may come before the celebrant, who lays hands on them individually. These prayers may be omitted; catechumens may be dismissed without an exorcism or prayer.

371. The RCIA does not say where the catechumens go. It implies that they simply leave. By recent custom, though, they are dismissed into a catechetical session to continue their formation. In some parishes a catechist steps forward, picks up the Lectionary or Book of the Gospels from wherever it was placed and leads a procession out of the church. *318, 353* Catechists are to take an active part in the rites of initiation (16).

CREED

372. The assembly of the faithful proclaims together the Creed, the summary of their principal beliefs. It is also called the profession of faith (OM 18, 19; GIRM 67, 68, 137). The Creed responds to the word of God and calls to mind and confesses the great mysteries of the faith before they are celebrated in the Eucharist (GIRM 67).

373. The Creed is proclaimed on Sundays and solemnities, and "at particular celebrations of a more solemn character" (GIRM 68). The Creed is part of every Sunday liturgy of the year, even during Advent and Lent, when the *Glory to God* is omitted. Some presiders have omitted the Creed *243* at Masses that are too early, too long, or too hot, but it does not take that long to recite and should be part of every Sunday and solemnity.

374. The Creed may be omitted on a few occasions. At the Easter Vigil it is replaced by the renewal of baptismal promises. After the Second Vatican Council the same renewal has replaced the Creed at Masses in the United States on Easter Sunday morning. If the baptism of children or the sacrament of confirmation takes place at Mass on a Sunday or solemnity, the renewal of promises replaces the Creed (Rite of Baptism for Children 29.2c; Rite of Confirmation 31a). The Creed may be omitted during the Rite of Acceptance into the Order of Catechumens (RCIA 68), the Rite of Sending the Catechumens for Election (117), the Rite of Election (137), the Scrutinies (156, 170, 177), some optional rites for baptized

candidates (445, 472), and several combined rites for catechumens and candidates (529, 546, 561). But its inclusion on Sundays is always appropriate. The post-Vatican II Missal explicitly stated that the Creed is not proclaimed on weekdays during the octave of Easter, even though they are all solemnities. The 2002 Missal omits that rubric, implying that the Creed is proclaimed on weekdays throughout the Easter octave.

375. The assembly normally proclaims the Nicene Creed (OM 18), but the Apostles' Creed may be used on some occasions (OM 19). The Apostles' Creed is older and was formulated from the questions asked those about to be baptized. The Nicene Creed summarizes the deeper reflection of the primitive Church.

376. The Apostles' Creed is appropriate for Sunday Masses of Lent and Easter (OM 19) because it is the "baptismal Creed" of the Roman Church (OM 19). During the third week of Lent, the faithful present the Creed to the elect for their reflection (RCIA 160). On Holy Saturday morning the elect proclaim the Creed back to the assembled faithful (196). Either Creed may be used, but the Apostles' Creed prepares people more directly for the questions they will hear at the Easter Vigil. On that night the elect are asked if they believe the Creed, part by part (225), and the faithful renew their baptismal promises (237). Therefore, at the Sunday Masses of Lent everyone may proclaim the Apostles' Creed because of its baptismal origins, even though the elect are dismissed before the Creed (OM 19). At Sunday Masses of the Easter season, the newly baptized take their places among the faithful, and all may proclaim the Apostles' Creed (OM 19).

377. The Apostles' Creed is also appropriate for Masses with children because those baptized as infants are expected to learn it in their catechetical formation (DMC 49). If it is used, children should still learn the phrases of the Nicene Creed little by little (39).

378. Children may sing an approved version of the Creed with words that do not exactly correspond to the liturgical texts (DMC 31; IOM 65).

379. The GIRM does not explicitly say where the priest is for the Creed, but the logical place is his chair. The proclamation of the Creed is not listed among the uses of the ambo (309).

380. All stand to proclaim the Creed (GIRM 43, 137). If people do not stand at the appropriate time, a deacon or the presider could gesture for them to rise. This will avoid a verbal instruction.

381. The Creed is to be proclaimed by the priest together with the people or by the people alternating with the choir (GIRM 68, 137). There is no provision for the choir singing the Creed alone. The OM supplies notes for singing the opening phrase of the Nicene Creed (18), as it does for the *Glory to God*. Traditionally the priest begins the Creed alone when it is sung, and the GIRM recommends this (68), but the opening musical phrase may be sung by a cantor or the choir instead. When it is spoken, the priest usually begins the Creed by default, although a cantor could cue it instead. Everyone could begin the Creed together if some minister gave a gesture of invitation. Some presiders introduce the text by saying something such as "Let us recite together the Creed." Indeed, if the Apostles' Creed is to be used during Lent and Easter, the people will need to know this before beginning; they may even need to know where to find the printed text in a participation aid. However, the fewer the words the better. If the people need to know which Creed to proclaim, the cantor, a song sheet, or hymn board could let them know. Otherwise, it is best not to give any other spoken introduction, but simply to begin the Creed. If someone begins the Creed by speaking the first words into a microphone, he or she should back away or switch it off once the people join in so that no single voice predominates.

382. Some presiders start the Creed while the assembly is still sitting, as if the first words mean "Please stand." One action should happen at a time. It is better to wait until everyone stands before starting the Creed.

383. During the Creed, at the words about the incarnation, all make a profound bow toward the altar (GIRM 137, 275b). The OM simply calls it a bow (18). This rubric is widely ignored by priest and faithful alike, although it was part of the liturgical books even before the 2002 revision. Prior to the Second Vatican Council, everyone genuflected at these words. The Council softened the rubric by calling for a profound bow, but many people do nothing at all. Surprising to many, the gesture is a profound bow, not a head bow, and is made in the direction of the altar. Depending on the location of the presider's chair, this may require him to turn his body as well. On the solemnities of the Annunciation of the Lord (March 25) and Christmas (December 25), the profound bow during the Creed is replaced with a genuflection (137). The IOM differs slightly, saying that all kneel on those two occasions (95). During the reading of the Passion on Palm Sunday and Good Friday, it is traditional for all to kneel for some moments of silence at the words of the death of Christ. To kneel at the words of the incarnation on the two principal days celebrating this mystery seems to fit

Catholic piety. Still, one does wonder why, out of all the truths proclaimed in the Creed, an accent is given to this particular one. The table of liturgical days ranks the Easter Triduum of the Lord's passion and resurrection ahead of the celebration of Christmas and other solemnities. Still, no tradition ever developed calling for the assembly to gesture in some way at the proclamation that Jesus rose again on the third day.

384.   It is recommended that the faithful sing the Creed (GIRM 68, 137), at least on occasion, and learn a setting in Latin (41). Very few assemblies have this ability. The people may sing in alternation with a cantor or the choir (68), which can facilitate the project.

622

385.   If the minister leading the petitions needs to move to a different place, it will cause less distraction if he or she does so immediately following the Creed, before the priest introduces the prayer of the faithful.

391

PRAYER OF THE FAITHFUL

Purpose and Nature

386.   The faithful exercise their priestly office by praying petitions for the needs of the Church and the world (OM 20; GIRM 69, 138). Usually the priest gives an introduction, petitions are named, the assembly responds after each one, and the priest concludes with a prayer.

387.   The composition of these texts is completely free. Most of the Catholic Mass is heavily scripted, but this prayer is designed to be freely composed church by church, Mass by Mass, so that particular needs may be brought to the attention of the community and commended to God. Samples can be found in the fifth appendix of the Missal. These are arranged by season of the year, and they include a set for Masses for the dead. Many Catholic publishing agencies offer sample prayers in print or on websites. The LM suggests that the priest's introduction and concluding prayer draw on the Scriptures of the day and the homily (43). Many priests improvise these texts, and some fall into patterns that feel safe by repetition. Careful preparation, however, will bring timely issues to the prayer of the faithful artfully composed (cf. GIRM 71).

Ministries

388.   The priest leads the introduction from his chair (GIRM 71, 138; LM 31). The 2002 GIRM instructs him to say these words with his hands

joined (138). The priest addresses the assembly, not God (IOM 98). His words may be based on the Scriptures of the day or the homily (LM 43). It would not be accurate for him to say, "Let us pray." More precisely, his introduction is an invitation to present petitions. The petitioner will invite people to pray. 255

389. The petitions are led by a deacon, cantor, lector, or any layperson (GIRM 71, 138, 171d, 197; LM 53). They are not to be led by a priest when someone else is available. When a deacon is present, he normally announces the intentions (GIRM 177; IOM 13; LM 50), but this does not prohibit another minister from doing so. If the deacon is active in parish ministries and attuned to the needs of society, hearing the petitions from him will especially suit his ministry. Often at papal Masses the intentions are divided among petitioners representing different nationalities, who each read one in his or her own language. 797

390. When children are present, they may illustrate the petitions with their artwork (DMC 36). In practice, the petitions are often divided among several speakers at Masses for children, in order to increase the number of people participating, but this sometimes causes more distraction than prayer.

LOCATION

391. The petitions are to be delivered from the ambo or another suitable place (GIRM 71, 138, 197). The LM had envisioned only the use of the ambo (31). The choice of location depends on who leads them. The ambo is preferred, but if a cantor is singing the intentions, he or she might do so from the cantor stand. A deacon leading the intentions could stand at his chair. The intentions are announced "while facing the people" (GIRM 138). But this should be obvious. 73

INTENTIONS

392. The intentions are to treat four areas: the needs of the Church, public authorities and the salvation of the whole world, those burdened by any kind of difficulty, and the local community (GIRM 70). Beyond those guidelines the prayers are freely composed. In many parishes the final petition is for the dead and mentions the person for whom the Mass is offered. The variable nature of these prayers suggests that they take into account the circumstances of time and place, the real contemporary needs of the Church and the world on the day they are prayed. Still, 526 387

the intentions should not be politicized or controversial. "They should express the prayer of the entire community" (71).

393. Some parishes allow members of the faithful to offer intentions spontaneously. This has the advantage of surfacing the real needs of those gathered but risks a host of challenges from inappropriate content to inaudibility. Spontaneous prayers chance making public what someone else was keeping private. More practical is a thoughtfully prepared list of intentions, *88* secured in a binder or folder to lend visual dignity to the prayer.

394. If the people's response is unfamiliar, the petitioner may need to supply it before beginning the intentions; for example, "Please respond, *398* 'Have mercy on us.'"

395. The intentions are addressed to the assembly, not to God (IOM 98). The petitioner announces the intentions, and the people pray for them.

396. Each of the intentions usually concludes with a verbal cue such as "Let us pray to the Lord." This cue is completely variable. It could change with the seasons of the year, for example. In practice, some petitioners raise an arm to cue the people for their response.

141 397. The intentions may be sung (GIRM 40, 71; LM 31, 53). The composition of sung texts requires special care. Whoever prepares the intentions needs to choose words that sound melodious when chanted. Sample tones are given in the first appendix of the Missal.

Response

398. The people's response is also variable. Most commonly they make an invocation together after each intention, but they may pray in silence instead (GIRM 71; LM 31). The response is addressed to God (IOM 98). It is this invocation or silent prayer that gives the prayer of the faithful its name. The importance of the people's prayer at this point cannot be overstressed. To enhance the spirit of prayer, some petitioners allow a moment of silence after each petition before giving the verbal cue for the people's response. It is important that all the baptized exercise their priestly function and be at prayer throughout this rite. One reason the catechumens are dismissed earlier is that this rite is properly the function *368* of the baptized (GIRM 69).

399. If the people's response is silence, the petitioner should allow for the silence to happen. In practice, though, people find it easier to participate

if they have a response to sing or say. Silence may make some feel that they have been asked not to participate. But a community comfortable with silent prayer may find such moments at Mass satisfying.

400. After the last response the petitioner's role is done. He or she may need to move from one place to another, for example, from the ambo to a pew. It will cause less distraction if the petitioner remains still until after the priest's concluding prayer (IOM 96).

CONCLUDING PRAYER

401. The priest offers an oration to conclude the intentions (GIRM 71). It is, of course, addressed to God. In summary, the priest introduces this rite by addressing the people; the petitioner announces the intentions addressing the people; the people respond addressing God; and the priest concludes addressing God. The priest extends his hands for the prayer (GIRM 138).

263

402. The words of this prayer may be freely composed or improvised. The LM recommends connecting it to the Scriptures or the homily (43). Presumably this prayer openly asks God to hear the foregoing petitions. Among the presidential prayers, the formula that concludes the collect (GIRM 54) is Trinitarian and longer than the one that concludes the prayer over the offerings (77) and the prayer after Communion (89). Logically, this presidential prayer will also use the shorter ending.

267, 513, 793

403. Following the prayer, the petitioner returns to his or her place if the intentions were announced away from there. If the petitioner leaves the sanctuary, it would be proper for him or her to make a profound bow to the altar (CB 72).

404. After this prayer all are seated (GIRM 43, 139), except those ministers who prepare the altar and the gifts.

405. If the priest is wearing a wireless microphone, switching it off after the prayer will eliminate some distractions.

Liturgy of the Eucharist

406. At the Last Supper Jesus took bread, blessed it, broke it and gave it to his disciples. He also blessed a cup of wine and gave it to them. "This is my body," he said. "This is my blood. Do this in memory of me." In the Liturgy of the Eucharist the Church prepares the gifts, gives thanks to God, breaks the bread, and shares Communion (GIRM 72).

PRELIMINARIES

407. If children have celebrated the Liturgy of the Word apart from the nave, they are brought back to the full assembly for the Liturgy of the Eu-
270, 404 charist (DMC 17). As everyone changes posture from standing to sitting, the children too find their places.

OFFERTORY CHANT

408. The offertory chant begins at the conclusion of the prayer of the
838 faithful (OM 21; GIRM 74, 139). It is optional.

409. If the people are to sing, the cantor may need to announce the song and invite participation. If some explanation of a special collection would be helpful, the cantor could also announce its purpose. No provision is made for such announcements (GIRM 31), but they would be useful for some practical details.

410. The norms for the manner of singing are the same as those for the entrance chant (74, cf. 48)—it involves the cantor, the choir, the people, or some combination of those resources. GIRM 48 names several sources for the text of the entrance antiphon: the Roman Missal, the Roman Gradual,
136–139 the Simple Gradual, or a song approved by bishops. But GIRM 74 fails to mention that the Roman Missal contains no text for the offertory chant, except on one occasion in the entire liturgical year, namely, Holy Thursday. Otherwise, the recommended texts for the offertory chant come from little used Latin books: the *Graduale Romanum* and the *Graduale Simplex*, and English translations such as *By Flowing Waters*. The offertories of the

Graduale Romanum are meticulously composed chant settings of verses drawn from a psalm or canticle. The offertories of the *Graduale Simplex* are musically less challenging; a short antiphon from a psalm or canticle alternates with several verses.

703

411. The GIRM now says "singing may always accompany" the preparation of the gifts, even if there is no procession (74). This new clarification replaces a statement in the pre-2002 GIRM that the offertory antiphon is omitted if it is not sung (50). As liturgical changes were happening with the Second Vatican Council, many parishes started singing four hymns at Mass: entrance, offertory, Communion, and closing. The pre-2002 GIRM deemphasized the significance of singing the offertory. The 2002 GIRM, though, preserved the tradition, without requiring it.

412. In place of singing, the organ may play instrumental music (cf. GIRM 142). Instruments are not to play solos during Lent, except on the *705* Fourth Sunday, solemnities, and feasts (GIRM 313). In practice, there *124* may also be no music at all.

413. The offertory music accompanies liturgical action (GIRM 37b). The music is meant to cease when the action does. The GIRM says that music may begin when the gifts are brought to the altar (74), whether they are brought forward from the back of the church by members of the faithful or from the credence table by servers. But if a collection precedes the procession of the gifts, the IOM sensibly says that music may begin with the collection (105). The music is to last until the gifts are placed on the altar, but in practice it often continues longer. A song with a refrain and *456, 481,* verses can easily be ended at the appropriate time. *499*

COLLECTION

414. One way the faithful express their participation at Mass is by offering gifts for the needs of the Church and the poor (OM 22; GIRM 73). Usually ushers collect the contributions (GIRM 105c). Some people arrange *41* for automatic deductions for the parish from their bank accounts, which assures a more steady flow of income for the parish but bypasses the ritual action of giving. Taking up a collection is always appropriate.

415. Customarily, each usher hands a basket to someone seated on the aisle. That person contributes and passes the basket to the next person, who does the same until the basket reaches the other end. An usher retrieves the basket and starts it down the next row. Alternatively, ushers

may stand at the aisles where they extend and retrieve baskets attached to long handles. Some find this expedient; others, distrustful. No legislation governs the method of collecting.

416. The Catholic Church takes up second collections for various global, national, and local needs. Baskets are often passed a second time for separate contributions for these specific purposes. It is common to take up the second collection after Communion, but this disturbs the flow of the liturgy. The time for offering contributions is during the preparation of the gifts. The second offering is more expressive if it is taken up at this time, a sign of the giver's participation in the sacrifice. The second collection may begin once the first is underway. Some parishes use a separate set of ushers and distinguishable baskets for the second collection. No legislation promotes taking up the second collection after Communion.

417. Other items may be collected on certain days—food for the local pantry; mittens, socks, and other gifts for the poor at Christmas; or back-to-school articles for needy children, for example. Besides the bread and wine, the offering of the faithful may be "other gifts for the relief of the needs of the Church and of the poor" (GIRM 140). In some parishes people may place these items at the door of the church when they enter, before taking their places. All these, or a selection of them, may be brought forward in the procession. In other parishes people may bring such special gifts forward to a designated place in the sanctuary as part of the collection. RS, however, takes a negative view of such donations: "Except for money and occasionally a minimal symbolic portion of other gifts, it is preferable that such offerings be made outside the celebration of Mass" (70).

418. While the collection is taken up, the priest and ministers remain seated and wait (IOM 105). In some parishes the collection has been starting with the Creed or the prayer of the faithful, or the ministers continue with the preparation of the gifts and even the Eucharistic Prayer while the collection is still underway. It is best if other liturgical actions cease during the collection so that everyone may give full attention to each part of the Mass. The preparation of the altar, however, needs no special attention and could take place during the collection without distraction.

PREPARING THE ALTAR

419. Ministers set the corporal, purificator, chalice, pall, and Missal on the altar (OM 21; GIRM 139). Prior to this time the altar should be clear

of these items (GIRM 306). "It is the deacon's place to take care of the sacred vessels himself" (178; cf. 171b), assisted by other ministers, but in his absence the acolyte or servers may bring these items to the altar (190). The priest remains at the chair.

71

650

420. There are exceptions. More than one corporal may be placed on the altar if Communion is to be offered from several chalices and ciboria. Additional chalices for the Communion of the faithful are set upon the corporals (NDR 36). The use of the pall is optional (GIRM 118c, 142; cf. 73), so it may be omitted. The chalice is not brought to the altar at this time if it is prepared at the credence table (73). Some priests prop the Missal on a pillow or bookstand for better visibility. There is no mention of it in the documents, but if one is to be used, it is brought to the altar at this time and set beneath the Missal.

99, 107
109

114.d,
651

421. Traditionally the Missal was placed slightly left of center, off the corporal, and angled toward the priest, who read from it with his head turned to the left. That tradition began when the priest celebrated Mass with his back to the people, facing an altar fixed on the rear wall. The shallow altar provided space for the chalice and paten in front of him, but the book had to sit at the side. When the altar became deeper and freestanding, many priests facing the people still placed the book and chalice in the same relationship, side by side. It is not necessary anymore, and it turns the face of the priest at an odd angle from the faithful. Some priests set the book immediately in front of them, centered on the altar, with the corporal and vessels behind the book and toward the faithful. The faithful then see the vessels, and the priest can more easily maintain eye contact with them when appropriate. With this arrangement the deacon can more easily assist with the book as needed (GIRM 171b). There are no rubrics governing the precise placement of the Missal on the altar.

422. In some churches the paten with a large host is placed on the altar together with the chalice. However, the GIRM does not call for it at this time. All the bread is brought forward with the wine after the altar has been prepared.

PROCESSION OF THE GIFTS

423. The faithful may demonstrate their participation in the Eucharist by bringing bread and wine to the altar, together with gifts for the church and the poor (OM 22; GIRM 140).

115

GIFTS

424. Bread, wine, and money or other gifts for the poor or for the Church are brought to the altar (GIRM 73). These are the primary symbols of the Eucharistic liturgy: the bread and wine will be transformed into the Body and Blood of Christ; the gifts for the Church and the poor are symbols of the sacrifice made by the entire assembly, who will also be transformed *516* by partaking in sacramental Communion.

425. The list of items in OM 22 and GIRM 73 does not include water. GIRM 72.1 says "wine with water" is brought to the altar "at the Preparation of the Gifts," but this presumes the circumstance where the chalice is prepared at the side table and brought to the altar with the water already mixed in the wine (73). The preparation of the gifts follows the procession of the gifts. However, 118c says the bread and cruets containing wine and water are placed on the credence table before Mass, "unless all of these are presented by the faithful in procession at the Offertory." Surely this is an oversight. The water cruet should not be brought forward in procession. In some parishes the procession erroneously includes the towel and bowl for washing the priest's hands. This is to be a procession *114* of gifts, not a setting of the credence table.

426. DMC 34 says, "The procession of children with the chalice and the gifts expresses more clearly the value and meaning of the preparation of the gifts." Perhaps a child could bring the prepared chalice from the credence table to the altar, but the chalice does not belong in the procession of the gifts.

427. IOM 105 says the procession should not include "token items that will be retrieved and returned to ordinary use after the celebration." At some school Masses, for example, students are invited to bring forward academic and sports insignia, but these do not belong in the procession of the gifts. They could be part of the ornamentation of the space before *125, 417* the liturgy begins (DMC 22, 29).

BREAD

Appearance

428. The bread should look like food. "The meaning of the sign demands that the material for the Eucharistic celebration truly have the appearance *648* of food" (GIRM 321).

429. The ingredients for Eucharistic bread are wheat and water. "The bread for celebrating the Eucharist must be made only from wheat, must be recently baked, and, according to the ancient tradition of the Latin Church, must be unleavened" (GIRM 320).

430. Low-gluten hosts may be used for the Eucharist, but not hosts that are completely gluten-free. With permission of the local bishop, low-gluten hosts may be made available for those who can tolerate only the smallest amount of gluten (Congregation for Doctrine of the Faith, Prot. 89/78–174, 98). To preserve their quality, they must be prepared in a vessel completely separate from the regular hosts. Those who cannot tolerate any gluten at all may receive from the cup instead, before others have done so.   *443*

431. In the past the people participating at Mass supplied the bread and wine (cf. IOM 104). The custom is still acknowledged in OM 22 and GIRM 140, which speak of the offering of the faithful: bread and wine or gifts for the Church and the poor. This rubric equates the offering of financial resources with the offering of the bread and wine, as if the faithful were responsible for bringing all of it along.

432. Some parishes have taken to heart the desire that Eucharistic bread "must be recently baked" (GIRM 320) and recruit members for this task. The processed wheat flour should not include other grains "to such an extent that [the result] would not commonly be considered wheat bread" (RS 48). Other substances, such as leaven, fruit, sugar, or honey may not be introduced into the making of bread for the Eucharist (GIRM 321; RS 48). Those who bake should be distinguished by their integrity, skilled in baking, and furnished with suitable tools (RS 48). Baked bread must be kept "in a perfect state of conservation"; it should not be allowed to "spoil or become too hard to be broken easily" (GIRM 323).

Hosts

433. Today most churches order bread for the Mass from companies or religious communities that make it in the form of hosts. Hosts have the appearance of food, but they resemble crackers more than bread. "Even though the faithful no longer bring from their own possessions the bread and wine intended for the liturgy as in the past, nevertheless the rite of carrying up the offerings still retains its force and its spiritual significance" (GIRM 73).

434. The GIRM promotes the "traditional shape" of bread (321), presumably as hosts. The IOM says the bread should be identifiable "by means of

its consistency—that is, its color, taste, texture, and smell—while its form should remain the traditional one" (50). The same paragraph says that the elements of the Eucharist follow an "unvarying tradition," but there have been exceptions: 104 acknowledged that "in the past, the people themselves provided the materials for the Eucharist," and GIRM 285b says hosts used for Communion by intinction should be "a little thicker than usual."

741

Size

435.   The bread should be large enough to be broken into several pieces "for distribution to at least some of the faithful" (GIRM 321). The permission (OM 130) for the *Lamb of God* to be "repeated as many times as necessary until the rite has reached its conclusion" presumes that the breaking of bread will take some time (GIRM 83). Later, when Communion is shared, "the faithful, though they are many, receive from the one bread the Lord's Body" (72.3). "The regular use of larger breads will foster an awareness of the fundamental symbolism in which all, priest and people, share in the same host. At every Mass at least one large host is broken into several portions" (IOM 131). Whenever the number of communicants is fairly small, it is possible to use one or more large hosts for the entire assembly to foster an awareness of unity.

661

436.   Most parishes use one large host and many small hosts. "Small hosts are, however, in no way ruled out when the number of those receiving Holy Communion or other pastoral needs require it" (GIRM 321). Small hosts are convenient and minimize crumbs, but they are essentially bread that is broken outside the context of the Eucharist, and they represent individuality more than unity. Still, RS 49 says, "Small hosts requiring no further fraction ought customarily to be used for the most part," but this will not obtain the "sign of unity" and the "sign of charity" envisioned by the breaking of the bread (GIRM 321). "The natural, the practical, the symbolic, and the spiritual are all inextricably linked in this most powerful symbol. Just as many grains of wheat are ground, kneaded, and baked together to become one loaf, which is then broken and shared out among many to bring them into one table-fellowship, so those gathered are made one body in the one bread of life that is Christ (see 1 Cor 10:17)" (IOM 130).

Quantity and Vessels

437.   The quantity should allow everyone to receive from the bread consecrated at the Mass they attend. "It is most desirable that the faithful

. . . receive the Lord's Body from hosts consecrated at the same Mass" (GIRM 85). The bread to be prepared for Mass is "for the Communion of the priest who presides, the deacon, the ministers, and the people" (118c). Many churches ignore these rubrics, however, and prepare only a host for the priest or hosts for some of the faithful, relying on previously consecrated hosts in the tabernacle for the Communion of the rest.   *114, 115, 663*

438. The bread is carried on a paten or in several ciboria (GIRM 118c; 306). Several ciboria are permitted, but a single vessel for the bread heightens the symbol of unity and permits the dividing of the consecrated bread into ciboria during the *Lamb of God*. "If possible, the bread and wine should each be contained in a single vessel, so that priest and people may be seen to be sharing the same food and drink in the sacrament of unity" (IOM 105). However, if there is no deacon, the priest will lift the chalice and the paten during the doxology, so he will need a bread vessel light enough to be elevated with one hand. Many priests retain the practice of placing one large host for themselves on a paten, and the bread for everyone else in a separate vessel. This tradition developed at a time when the faithful did not receive Communion at Mass, or if they did, they were given Communion from a ciborium in the tabernacle. Today the practice of separate bread vessels for the priest and the people does not adequately symbolize the sacrament of unity.   *460*   *102*   *652*   *606*

WINE

439. The wine must come from grapes. "The wine for the Eucharistic celebration must be from the fruit of the grapevine (cf. Lk 22:18), natural, and unadulterated, that is, without admixture of extraneous substances" (GIRM 322).

440. The wine should be "kept in a perfect state of conservation"; it should not be allowed to turn to vinegar (GIRM 323).

441. Mustum, "which is grape juice that is either fresh or preserved by methods that suspend its fermentation without altering its nature (for example, freezing)," may be used for the Eucharist. The local bishop may approve it for clergy or laypersons who cannot drink alcohol (Congregation for Doctrine of the Faith, Prot. 89/78–174, 98).

442. If Communion is offered to the faithful under both forms, a sufficient quantity of wine should be prepared. "It is most desirable that the faithful . . . in the instances when it is permitted . . . partake of the

chalice (cf. no. 283), so that even by means of the signs Communion will stand out more clearly as a participation in the sacrifice actually being celebrated" (GIRM 85).

720

443. Still, the communicant who receives under only one form partakes fully in Communion. "Christ, whole and entire, and the true Sacrament, is received even under only one species, and . . . those who receive under only one species are not deprived of any of the grace that is necessary for salvation" (GIRM 282). When Communion is distributed under both kinds, "any of the faithful who wish to receive Holy Communion under the species of bread alone should be granted their wish" (284). A layperson afflicted with celiac disease, who is unable to receive Communion under any form of bread, may receive under the form of wine only (Congregation for Doctrine of the Faith, Prot. 89/78–174, 98).

430

444. RS suggests that the chalice might not be offered "where a notable part of the people continues to prefer not to approach the chalice for various reasons, so that the sign of unity would in some sense be negated" (102). However, catechesis on the Eucharistic banquet, the new and eternal covenant, and the eschatological banquet (cf. GIRM 281) could also be given to encourage participation.

445. Some of the Precious Blood may be temporarily reserved for sick people unable to attend the Eucharist (PCS 74). Their participation should also be considered in preparing the quantity of wine for the Eucharist. For carrying Communion, a sacred vessel resembling a flask or jar works well. If the opening is narrow, making it difficult to pour wine into it during the Mass, it would be better to bring it to the altar filled.

469, 755

446. The quantity of wine prepared, then, should invite participation. The GIRM says that care should be taken "lest beyond what is needed of the Blood of Christ remains to be consumed at the end of the celebration" (285a). Common sense, Christian courtesy, and the meaning of signs suggest that similar care should be taken that enough is prepared for all who wish to partake. Those coming last in the Communion line still deserve the option of receiving under both forms. The GIRM provides for the consumption of any consecrated wine that remains after Communion (163).

115, 757

447. If the wine is brought forward in a single vessel, "priest and people may be seen to be sharing the same . . . drink in the sacrament of unity" (IOM 105). The use of one chalice at Communion would signify the sharing of the Lord's Blood "in the same way the Apostles received . . . from Christ's own hands" (GIRM 72.3), but the number of people in attendance

at Mass makes this impractical. Although flagons are not to be used for consecrated wine (RS 106), one or more may be used to carry the wine to the altar for the preparation of the gifts.

103

PROCESSION

448. The gifts are brought forward. The servers and deacon or other ministers may bring the bread and wine from the credence table to the priest at the altar, especially at simple celebrations (GIRM 190, 100). But *115* it is recommended that members of the faithful bring the gifts to the sanctuary (OM 22; GIRM 73, 140). "The congregation's identification with the gifts is best expressed if the procession passes right through their midst" (IOM 105).

449. Those who bring the gifts forward are identified as "the faithful" (OM 22; GIRM 73; IOM 101). The few who bring the gifts represent the many who provide them. Implicitly, "the faithful" will also receive back the bread and wine transformed as the Body and Blood of Christ. In practice, though, some communities encourage those who will not receive Communion—very young children or non-Catholics—to bring forward the gifts in order to include them in the celebration. However, this is like asking someone to provide food for a dinner they will attend but not eat. At children's Masses, admittedly, having children bring forward the gifts is encouraged (DMC 18). This procession of children "expresses more clearly the value and meaning of the preparation of the gifts" (DMC 34), presumably as a sign of their offering, unless the Directory also assumes that these children are old enough to share Communion.

450. At special celebrations servers bearing candles may accompany the procession of the gifts (IOM 22). Ushers may assist with the procession (23), and many do so by handing items to those who will bring them to the sanctuary and by sending the participants forward in an orderly way. The documents do not propose a sequence for these gifts. Many processions are ordered the way the documents describe the gifts: bread, wine, and then gifts for the Church and the poor. The gifts may also arrive in the reverse order, permitting the priest to receive the bread last and proceed immediately to the prayer of praise for it.

457

451. After the bearers have presented their gifts, it would be appropriate for them to make a profound bow to the altar. If ministers stand between the bearers and the altar to receive the gifts, the bearers logically wait to bow until the ministers have cleared their view of the altar. The documents

do not explicitly state what if any sign of reverence should be given at this point. A genuflection is made at the beginning and end, not during Mass, and only when the tabernacle is in the sanctuary (GIRM 274). A profound bow is made to the altar by all who pass before it (CB 72). In practice, some people bearing gifts bow to the ministers, make the sign of the cross, or inappropriately genuflect to the altar before or after handing over the gifts. Others make no sign of reverence. The suitable reverence would be a profound bow to the altar just before returning to their places. No words need to be exchanged, but at papal Masses some brief conversation has been observed, and the pope has traced the sign of the cross on the foreheads of those who have carried forward the gifts.

PREPARATION OF THE GIFTS

RECEIVING THE GIFTS

452. The gifts are received from the faithful "at an appropriate place" (GIRM 73, 178). Usually this is the front of the sanctuary, but it could also be at the altar.

453. Either the priest or the deacon may receive the gifts (GIRM 73, 178). Other ministers may assist (140). The IOM says less precisely, "The gifts are accepted by the priest, who may be assisted by the deacon and other ministers" (105). But the priest may remain at the chair while the deacon receives the gifts from the faithful. If there are more vessels than the priest and/or deacon can carry, he or they may receive the gifts from those bearing them and hand them to other ministers, who will bring them to the priest when he arrives at the altar.

454. Ideally, there will be one collection basket, one vessel for bread, and another vessel for wine. If there are additional vessels, they could be carried on a tray. Out of respect for the vessels, ministers should not carry more than two each, even if it requires more ministers or more than one trip to the altar.

455. The priest does not lift up the collection as he does the bread and wine. Rather, it is put "in a suitable place but away from the Eucharistic table" (GIRM 73, 140). The "table" means the top of the altar. The same Latin word used here for table, *mensa*, is left untranslated elsewhere in the English GIRM (304, 305, 306). Some parishes place the collection on the floor in front of the altar or on a low table in the sanctuary. Others place it immediately in a safe or entrust it to ushers for counting during

460, 475

the Mass, even sending an empty basket to the altar together with the bread and wine. But these solutions inhibit the point of the offering and procession, which symbolize the sacrifice of the lives of the faithful, to be transformed in the sanctuary at this Eucharist. The collection should be visible, but never on top of the altar.

828

456. If there is an offertory song, it continues at least until the gifts are placed on the altar (GIRM 74). In practice, though, some parishes end the music about the time when the gifts have been received or continue till the washing of the hands.

413, 481, 499

TAKING THE BREAD

457. At the altar the priest receives the bread and wine. He may receive them directly from those bearing them or from assistant ministers. The acolyte or servers may hand the bread and wine to the priest at the altar (GIRM 190, 100); if there is a deacon, he does so (178). But if the priest received the gifts at the front of the sanctuary, he may have carried at least the bread to the altar himself. In practice, servers may place the bread and wine on the altar for the priest, but the placement of the elements on the altar is a significant moment of the Mass, and the action is part of the priest's responsibilities.

450

458. The celebrant places the bread and wine on the altar (GIRM 140) "to the accompaniment of the prescribed formulas" (75). There appear to be two options here. He may place the bread and wine on the altar as soon as he arrives there, for convenience. Or he may receive them one by one and place them on the altar as he says the respective formulas pertaining to the bread and the wine. This option works better if a deacon has prepared the wine at the credence table (178).

459. If the priest will be reciting the next prayers aloud, and if he is wearing a wireless microphone, he switches it on before taking the bread.

462

460. The priest, standing at the altar, takes the paten with the bread (OM 23; GIRM 141). Logically, if the bread for the entire assembly has been carried to the altar in one larger paten, ciborium, or bowl, that is the vessel he holds.

438

461. The priest holds the vessel of bread slightly above the altar with both hands (OM 23; GIRM 141). He does not lift the vessel very high. An elevation will come later in the Mass. Here he is taking the bread as Jesus took bread on the night before he died.

475, 606

462. Holding the vessel, the priest prays a text that blesses God for the bread (OM 23; GIRM 141). He recites this formula quietly if the offertory chant is being sung or if "the organ" (or logically, another instrument) is being played, but he may say it aloud if there is no music (GIRM 142). He may also say it quietly if there is no music, but that is not its purpose. In practice, some priests wait until the music is over before beginning these prayers or proclaim them in a very loud voice over the music as it continues. But these prayers may be said quietly, and they probably should be in those circumstances. The IOM interprets "quietly" to mean "inaudibly" (106). It should appear that the priest is praying, not whispering secrets.

463. If there is no music at this time and the priest has recited the formula aloud, the people respond, "Blessed be God for ever" (OM 23; GIRM 142). This acclamation is omitted when the priest recites the text silently. The OM places this acclamation after the priest has set the vessel of bread down, but the words of the people will be more sensibly joined to those of the priest if he holds the vessel off the altar until they have made their acclamation.

464. The priest places the vessel of bread on the corporal (OM 23; GIRM 141). Ideally, this is the first time the bread is actually placed on the altar (GIRM 306). It goes there only after God has been praised for it.

ADDING WATER

465. The deacon or the priest pours wine and a little water into the chalice (OM 24; GIRM 142).

466. If there is a deacon, he may perform this action at the credence table (GIRM 178). If there is no deacon, the servers or other ministers bring the wine and water to the side of the altar, where the priest mixes the liquids (142). The IOM implies that even the priest may prepare the chalice at the credence table (107), but the GIRM does not explicitly state this, and a priest moving from the altar to the credence table would draw too much attention to the adding of water. This action takes place away from the middle of the altar to show its secondary nature. The GIRM actually says, ". . . the minister presents the cruets" (142), but there is no need for a wine cruet if another minister has brought the wine forward in another vessel.

467. If the cruets have lids, a minister needs to remove and replace them. Lids offer little value and add unnecessary actions. The documents are silent on lids.

468. If one chalice is not sufficient for Communion, a minister pours the wine into all the cups on the corporal (NDR 36). After the Second Vatican Council, the approved practice was to consecrate wine in the flagon first and then pour it into the cups during the breaking of the bread. RS changed this legislation: "The pouring of the Blood of Christ after the consecration from one vessel to another is completely to be avoided, lest anything should happen that would be to the detriment of so great a mystery. Never to be used for containing the Blood of the Lord are flagons, bowls, or other vessels that are not fully in accord with the established norms" (106). In parishes with many Communion stations, this has introduced a delay. Some bishops have permitted a variance. *99*

103

469. If Communion is to be brought to the sick under the form of wine (PCS 74), an appropriate vessel should be prepared also, in order to avoid pouring after the consecration (RS 106). If the container is small, filling it before Mass will eliminate the danger of spilling. This vessel would appropriately remain open during the Mass; a minister could screw the lid on after Communion. *445, 755*

470. The amount of water is described only as "a little" (OM 24; GIRM 142). Most clergy add a few drops. The deacon or priest may wipe the spout of the water cruet with a purificator for neatness, but this is not in the rubrics.

471. The water is added to the wine in "the chalice" (OM 24; GIRM 142), but neither of these texts presumes that there might be a larger container of wine or several chalices for the Communion of the faithful. Water may be added to the wine in one chalice, but that diminishes the symbol. There is no legislation against adding the water to a single flagon of wine before pouring the cups, a solution that is practical if the flagon already rests on the altar and if the opening is wide enough that water can be added without the aid of a funnel. As the spoken text will make clear, the primary symbol here is the mixing of wine and water, not the use of the chalice. Alternatively, if the wine is poured first, no legislation forbids pouring water into more than one chalice. Whatever solution is chosen, this is a secondary action that should not attract much attention.

472. While adding water to the wine, the deacon or priest recites a prayer that the people may share in the divinity of Christ, who shared in their humanity (OM 24; GIRM 142, 178). Even though the prayer uses the first person plural, it is spoken quietly. Even if there is no music and if the priest recites the blessing prayers of the bread and wine aloud, the

deacon or priest still says this text quietly (GIRM 33). The IOM says this text is to be recited "inaudibly" (107); the quiet prayer of the priest or deacon "allows the faithful to pray silently in their own way during these moments" (39).

473. If a server has brought the water to the altar, the priest or deacon who adds water to the wine hands the water back to the server. In practice, they sometimes bow to each other, but there is no rubric that this should be done.

TAKING THE CUP

474. If the priest prepared the wine at the side of the altar, he moves to the middle of the altar (GIRM 142). He has never moved from the middle if the deacon has prepared the wine.

461, 606 475. The priest picks up the chalice with both hands, or the deacon hands it to him (OM 25; GIRM 142, 178). He holds the chalice a little above the altar, in the same way he held the bread, avoiding an elevation of the chalice.

476. Holding the vessel, the priest prays a text blessing God for the wine (OM 25; GIRM 142). He recites this formula quietly, even inaudibly (IOM 107) if the offertory chant is being sung or if the organ (or another instrument) is being played, but he may say it aloud if there is no music
462 (GIRM 142).

477. If the music ends between the taking of the bread and the taking of the cup, it is advisable for the priest to recite the second text quietly as well. He should not combine the two prayers into one. "The two blessings should be seen as a unit; for one to be said inaudibly and the other aloud should never happen, nor should the two be joined into one prayer" (IOM 106).

478. If there has been no music during the preparation of the gifts and the priest has recited the formula aloud, the people respond, "Blessed
463 be God for ever" (OM 25; GIRM 142). This acclamation is omitted when the priest recites the text silently. The OM places this acclamation after the priest has set the chalice down, but the words of the people will be more sensibly joined to those of the priest if he holds the vessel off the altar until they have made their acclamation.

479. The priest places the chalice on the corporal (OM 25; GIRM 142). As with the bread, ideally, this is the first time the wine is actually placed

on the altar. It goes there only after God has been praised for it. But this is hardly possible when multiple chalices are in use, or even with one, unless a deacon has prepared the wine at the credence table. The arrangement of multiple chalices will depend on the number of chalices, the size and shape of the altar, and the seating. Chalices should be arranged in a way that the principal chalice predominates. Sometimes it works best to place others on corporals on one or both sides of the altar. *458, 464* *466*

480. The priest may cover the chalice with a pall (GIRM 142), but this is optional (118c). It would also be impractical to cover many chalices with palls when Communion is prepared under both forms. *109, 578*

481. If an offertory chant is sung, it "continues at least until the gifts have been placed on the altar" (GIRM 74). The gifts are not formally placed on the altar until after the blessing prayers, and the rite of preparing the gifts still requires several more steps. In practice, the music usually covers at least the procession of the gifts to the sanctuary, if not the entire rite to the washing of the hands. *413, 456, 499*

Private Prayer

482. The priest makes a profound bow to the altar and recites quietly a prayer that God will receive the sacrifice (OM 26; GIRM 143).

483. The prayer is not said aloud. The priest prays "in his own name, asking that he may exercise his ministry with greater attention and devotion" (GIRM 33). This particular prayer is based on the one offered by Azariah in the fiery furnace (Daniel 3:39).

484. This is one of the moments in the Mass that calls for the priest to make a profound bow of the body (GIRM 275b).

Incensing the Gifts

485. The gifts, the cross, the altar, the priest, and the people may be incensed (OM 27; GIRM 276d). Incense may be used at any Mass, but it is recommended for special days. *153*

486. The thurifer, deacon, server, or another minister brings the boat containing incense and the thurible containing hot coals to the priest (GIRM 190). The thurifer usually hands the priest the boat and lifts the top of the thurible. The priest spoons incense into the thurible and blesses the smoke, making the sign of the cross with his hand but speaking no *354*

words (144, 277). He hands the boat to the thurifer, who gives him the thurible.

487. The priest does not make a profound bow (GIRM 277) but incenses the gifts immediately (75, 144). Normally a profound bow is made to the person or object being incensed both before and after an incensation. This instruction is new to the 2002 GIRM, but in the pre-Vatican II Missal the priest also omitted a reverence to the cross before incensing the gifts. Omitting the bow to the altar and the offerings minimizes the number of bows during this incensation.

488. To incense the offerings, the priest makes three swings of the thurible toward them, or he may make the sign of the cross over the offerings with the thurible (GIRM 277). He chooses one method or the other, not both. This instruction is new to the 2002 GIRM, but it greatly reduces the rather complicated method of incensing the gifts in the pre-Vatican II Missal.

489. The priest incenses the cross and the altar, again making no bow (GIRM 75, 144, 277). He swings the thurible three times toward the cross. He makes a number of single swings toward the altar as he walks around it. If the cross is not on or near the altar, the priest incenses it as he passes in front of it while circling the altar.

490. The deacon or acolyte may assist (178, 190), but the GIRM does not explain how. Traditionally he sets the boat on the credence table or the incense stand. He might hold the priest's vestments away from the smoke. But usually the priest can manage the incensation without additional assistance, and sometimes the minister just gets in the way.

491. The priest hands the thurible to the deacon or another minister at the side of the altar. That minister makes a profound bow to the priest and incenses him with three swings of the thurible (OM 27; GIRM 144, 178, 190, 277). The minister bows again. Some priests also bow to the thurifer, but there is no such instruction.

492. The minister with the incense then incenses the people (OM 27; GIRM 144, 178, 190, 277). Traditionally the thurifer stands between the altar and the people, but the GIRM does not say exactly where. The people stand (IOM 108). If they do not, it would be appropriate for the thurifer or deacon politely to gesture for them to do so. The thurifer makes a profound bow, swings the thurible three times, and bows again. In practice, if the assembly is spread through different parts of a large nave, the thurifer repeats this sequence for each section. Sometimes the people bow to the

thurifer, but that is not in the GIRM. They are the ones being incensed, and they receive the reverence of the thurifer.

WASHING HANDS

493. The priest washes his hands at the side of the altar to express his desire for interior purification (OM 28; GIRM 76, 145).

494. If incense is used, the priest often performs this action while the thurifer incenses the people. It is generally better not to let actions overlap, but in this case one concerns the people and the other concerns the priest, so the concurrence is not offensive.

495. The "side of the altar" is where the wine may be prepared (GIRM 142) and where the priest stands for his incensation (144). These actions are *466, 491* secondary and do not take place at the middle of the altar. Depending on the size of the altar and the space in the sanctuary, the priest might stand a bit apart from the altar for his incensation and the washing of his hands.

496. Traditionally servers pick up a pitcher, basin, and towel from the credence table (cf. GIRM 188c). One pours water over the priest's hands *114* (145). The GIRM never specifically mentions a basin and towel, but logically these will be needed. It usually goes more smoothly if the server *106* who pours also holds the basin. If there is only one server, he or she usually drapes the towel over the arm of the hand holding the basin. Some servers, probably inspired by the "little" water added from a cruet to the wine just moments before, pick up the same cruet and pour only a *468* few drops over the priest's hands into a finger bowl, while offering him a small white cloth, folded even smaller. But the IOM observes, "For the sake of authenticity, this action needs to be performed with dignity and deliberation. An appreciable quantity of water is poured from a pitcher, and the hands are dried with a towel" (109). The pitcher and basin should *111* be large enough to pour and receive this appreciable quantity (IOM 51). The server will help if he or she opens the towel all the way.

497. As the priest washes his hands, he recites quietly a text asking God to cleanse him of sin (OM 28; GIRM 145; IOM 109). It is one of the private prayers he offers to exercise his ministry with greater devotion (GIRM 33). He then dries his hands with the towel.

498. The priest hands the towel back to the server. In some parishes the priest and the servers bow to each other at this point, but there is no such rubric.

413, 456,
481

499. In practice, the music during the preparation of the gifts often ends after the washing of the hands, even though the GIRM only says it lasts at least until the bread and wine are set on the altar (74).

INVITATION AND RESPONSE

500. The priest invites the people to pray that God will find the sacrifice acceptable (OM 29; GIRM 146). The rubric notes that the priest stands at the middle of the altar and faces the people. It is important to say that he returns to the middle because he has just washed his hands at the side. But to indicate that he faces the people implies that the altar might be against the wall. The altar should be freestanding (GIRM 299).

67

501. In many parishes the assembly stands just before the priest says these words; in others the people rise after the invitation, as they begin to make their response. OM 29 and GIRM 146 say the people stand for their response, even though GIRM 43 indicates that they stand at the invitation. Humanly speaking, this dialogue makes more sense if everyone has the same posture throughout. In practice, congregations that stand as they respond end up speaking the first words while changing posture. It seems more natural if the people stand after the washing of the hands, just before the priest invites them to pray. If incense has been used, the entire assembly is already standing.

492

502. If the priest has recited the other texts of the preparation of the gifts silently and if he is wearing a wireless microphone, he switches it on for the invitation.

503. The priest extends and joins his hands while he speaks this text (OM 29; GIRM 146). This resembles the gesture he makes with the greeting in the introductory rites, the preface, the greeting of peace, and at the final blessing and is one reason why some priests feel that a similar gesture is appropriate for the invitation "Let us pray" at the collect and prayer after Communion.

202, 539,
631, 802
255, 786

504. At Masses with children the priest may give this invitation in his own words to "help him reach the hearts of the children" (DMC 23). But he needs to cue the children's response clearly or they won't know when to speak.

505. The people express their desire that the sacrifice may praise God's name and help the Church (OM 29; GIRM 146). This dialogue prepares the priest and people for the Eucharistic Prayer (GIRM 77).

506. Both the invitation and the response may be sung, though they rarely are. The singing of dialogues is encouraged (GIRM 40), and a sample chant appears in the first appendix of the Missal.

141

507. Some priests say "Amen" after the people have given their response. But that word does not appear here in the liturgy. The people's statement is not an oration, and the priest's only reply is to offer the next prayer.

PRAYER OVER THE OFFERINGS

508. The priest extends his hands and says the prayer over the offerings (OM 30; GIRM 77, 146). This prayer usually prepares for the Eucharistic Prayer by indicating the purpose for which these gifts have been brought.

509. The extension of hands indicates that the text is a prayer addressed to God.

263, 620, 788

510. On Sundays the text for this prayer comes from the Mass of the day. There is a wider choice of Masses on most weekdays. At Masses with children the priest may select a different prayer that better connects with them, preferably from the same liturgical season (DMC 50). He may even adapt the words of the prayer to make them more understandable to children (51). The GIRM notes that only one prayer is offered (77) because prior to the Council there were occasions when the priest said more than one.

261

262, 789

511. The Missal is resting on the altar. IOM 22 says, "Servers hold the book while the presiding priest proclaims the presidential prayers with outstretched hands," but that does not apply in this case.

512. If the text of this prayer specifies the saint(s) in whose honor Mass is being celebrated, "a bow of the head is made" (GIRM 275a) at the mention of the name(s). This probably refers to the presiding priest's head. A bow of the head is also made if the name of Jesus is mentioned in the concluding formula. Not all priests observe this rubric.

513. The people answer "Amen" to the short conclusion of the prayer (OM 30; GIRM 146), "uniting themselves to this entreaty" and making the prayer their own (GIRM 77).

267

514. The prayer and the Amen may be sung. The singing of such texts is encouraged (GIRM 40), and sample chants appear in the first appendix of the Missal.

141

EUCHARISTIC PRAYER

MEANING

515. The Eucharistic Prayer is the prayer of thanksgiving and sanctification. It is the center and summit of the entire celebration of the Mass (GIRM 78). In the Eucharistic Prayer the priest turns to God in the name of the whole people, gives thanks, and offers the living and holy sacrifice. He prays that the Body and Blood of Christ may be a sacrifice acceptable to the Father and salvific for the whole world (2). In the Eucharistic Prayer "the Body and Blood of Christ are made present by the power of the Holy Spirit," and "the people are joined to Christ in offering his sacrifice to the Father" (IOM 111). "The Church gives praise and thanks for God's holiness and justice and for all God's mighty deeds. . . . The Last Supper is recounted; the mystery of Christ's passion, saving death, resurrection, and ascension is recalled; the memorial sacrifice of his Body and Blood is offered to the Father; and the Holy Spirit is invoked to sanctify the gifts and transform those who partake of them into the Body of Christ, uniting them with the whole Church of God, living and dead, into one communion of love, service, and praise to the glory of the Father" (112).

516. Even though the priest proclaims most of the words of the prayer, "the meaning of the Prayer is that the entire congregation of the faithful should join itself with Christ in confessing the great deeds of God and in the offering of Sacrifice. The Eucharistic Prayer demands that all listen to it with reverence and in silence" (GIRM 78). "The people, for their part, should associate themselves with the priest in faith and in silence, as well as through their parts as prescribed in the course of the Eucharistic Prayer" (147). RS 52 overstates that "the Eucharistic Prayer, then, is to be recited by the Priest alone in full"; the dialogues and acclamations of the people are also part of the Eucharistic Prayer, which RS 54 acknowledges.

37, 424, 692

517. At children's Masses the importance of the prayer is made clear by the priest's manner of proclamation and by the children's attention and acclamations. "The disposition of mind required for this central part of the celebration and the calm and reverence with which everything is done must make the children as attentive as possible. Their attention should be on the real presence of Christ on the altar under the elements of bread and wine, on his offering, on the thanksgiving through him and with him and in him, and on the Church's offering, which is made during the prayer and by which the faithful offer themselves and their lives with Christ to the eternal Father in the Holy Spirit" (DMC 52).

518. The priest continues to stand at the middle of the altar. If there is a deacon, he "stands near the priest but slightly behind him, so that when needed he may assist the priest with the chalice or the Missal" (GIRM 179). Traditionally the deacon's liturgical ministry involved preparing, moving, and holding the chalice. At the end of the Eucharistic Prayer, he will lift the chalice. During the prayer some deacons turn the pages of the Missal so that the priest can keep his arms extended.

519. The priest may introduce and explain the Eucharistic Prayer in his own words (GIRM 31). This may be done before the preface dialogue, but not during the prayer. Such an introduction could name additional reasons for thanksgiving or point out connections between the readings of the day and the text of the prayer. But this particular introduction is rarely done, probably under the assumption that people grasp the basic meaning and significance of the Eucharistic Prayer and to avoid commentary that detracts from the spirit of prayer.

520. A deacon "guides the faithful by appropriate introductions and explanations" (GIRM 171d), so he could offer this introduction in place of the priest.

521. Even children could contribute to this introduction. At Masses with children their participation may be encouraged by "the insertion of motives for giving thanks before the priest begins the dialogue of the preface" (DMC 22).

CHOICE OF PRAYER

522. The Roman Missal includes four general Eucharistic Prayers, three more for Masses with children, and another two on the theme of reconciliation. There is also a Eucharistic Prayer for Masses for various needs and occasions, which comes in four variations. The priest selects one of these ten prayers for the Mass (GIRM 147). The GIRM comments only on the first four. The OM places these four within its body, suggesting the deference due to them. The Missal includes all the others, but strangely packaged in two separate appendices. The Eucharistic Prayers for Masses of reconciliation and of various needs and occasions appear in an appendix right after the OM, but the Eucharistic Prayers for Masses with children are somewhat concealed without tabs in the final appendix of the book. 85

523. Eucharistic Prayer I is also known by its former title, the Roman Canon (OM 83–98). It is believed to have come from Rome, and it served as the only Eucharistic Prayer in the Roman Rite for over a thousand years. For that reason it was the "canon," a word referring to its uniqueness. The other Eucharistic Prayers are not properly called canons.

524. Eucharistic Prayer I appears without a preface because its preface is completely variable. But the chosen preface becomes part of this Eucharistic Prayer. On days of special importance certain lines may be inserted into this prayer to speak of the reason for giving thanks (for example, the birth of Jesus) or the identity of some people present (for example, the newly baptized). After the Second Vatican Council, some lines of this prayer became optional, primarily to abbreviate its length (OM 32). Hence the two lists of saints may be shortened, lamentably eliminating the names of all women saints in the second group, and the many intermediate concluding doxologies may be omitted ("through Christ our Lord. Amen.").

557, 559, 596, 602

525. Eucharistic Prayer I may always be used, but it is especially appropriate on days when there is a proper text to be inserted (for example, the octave of Easter), when the Church celebrates one of the saints mentioned in the prayer, and on Sundays (GIRM 365a).

526. Eucharistic Prayer II was added to the Missal after the Council, but it is based on a text probably dating from third to fourth century Rome (OM 99–106). It enjoys some easy popularity because it is the briefest of the Eucharistic Prayers. It comes with its own preface, but it may be exchanged with another, especially one of the common prefaces, known in the post-Vatican II sacramentary as the prefaces for weekdays in Ordinary Time (OM 72–77). The prayer includes an optional formula to remember deceased persons by name in Masses for the dead. Many

392 parishes remember such persons as part of the prayer of the faithful.

527. Eucharistic Prayer II, because of its "particular features," is appropriate for weekdays "or in special circumstances" (GIRM 365b), though it is not clear what these features are. The prayer fits occasions that call for a proper preface, Masses for the dead, or times when brevity is desirable.

528. Eucharistic Prayer III is a new composition added to the Missal after the Second Vatican Council (OM 107–115). Like Eucharistic Prayer I, it has no preface of its own, but the preface chosen becomes part of

the Eucharistic Prayer. Like Eucharistic Prayer II, it contains an optional formula to name the deceased at Masses for the dead.

529. Eucharistic Prayer III "is preferred on Sundays and feast days" (GIRM 365c). It was composed as an alternative to Eucharistic Prayer I for these occasions.

530. Eucharistic Prayer IV was new to the Missal after Vatican II but is based on a much older prayer (OM 116–123). It carries its own preface, which may never be replaced with another because of its integration with the whole prayer.

531. Eucharistic Prayer IV "may be used when a Mass has no Preface of its own and on Sundays in Ordinary Time" (GIRM 365d). IOM 113 says all four of these prayers "are for use throughout the liturgical year," but Eucharistic Prayer IV is intended for Ordinary Time.

532. The two Eucharistic Prayers for Masses of reconciliation were offered to the Church in connection with the Jubilee Year of 1975. They begin with prefaces announcing the theme, but these may be replaced with other prefaces that refer to penance and conversion (cf. *Notitiae* 19 [1983] 270). "They are particularly appropriate for use during the season of Lent and may be used at other times when the mystery of reconciliation is reflected in the readings or other texts of the Mass" (IOM 113).

533. The Eucharistic Prayer for Masses for various needs and occasions comes with four variations of paired prefaces and intercessions. It is "particularly suited for use with formularies of the Masses for Various Needs and Occasions" (IOM 113). It is not prohibited at other times.

534. When many children are present, one of the Eucharistic Prayers for Masses with children may be used. "The Eucharistic Prayer which seems best suited to the needs of the children in each nation should be chosen from among the three texts: either the first for its greater simplicity, the second for its greater participation, or the third for the variations it affords" (Eucharistic Prayers for Masses with Children: Introduction, 15). 36

SINGING

535. In most churches the people's acclamations of the Eucharistic Prayer are sung. But the priest may sing the entire prayer (OM 32). "It is very appropriate that the priest sing those parts of the Eucharistic Prayer for which musical notation is provided" (GIRM 147). The singing of

dialogues and of texts common to the priest and people is encouraged (GIRM 40). The first appendix of the Missal contains a sample of the preface dialogue and two settings of the preface. Each of the four general Eucharistic Prayers contains notes for the memorial acclamation and the doxology with its Amen. Chant settings for these four prayers are found in the second section of the Missal after the Order of Mass. There are two for Eucharistic Prayer I—one common and the other more solemn. The solemn setting provides notes for the middle of the prayer and says the presider may sing the rest of the text from the common setting. In all these cases the entire prayer is set to music, not just the first half or the institution narrative, as the post-Vatican II Sacramentary had done for Eucharistic Prayer I. This implies that the presider sings the entire prayer, not just part of it. The Eucharistic Prayers for Masses with children include additional acclamations that may be sung throughout.

536. Since Vatican II some composers have written accompanied sung settings of the Eucharistic Prayers. The GIRM cautions that while the priest is speaking the presidential texts, "there should be no other prayers or singing, and the organ or other musical instruments should be silent" (32). This caution appeared in the postconciliar GIRM as well, so it did not refer to the practice composers developed later: instruments playing accompaniment for a singing presider. The caution refers to an earlier practice: before the Council the organist sometimes played solos during the Eucharistic Prayer, which was offered in Latin in a low voice. Solo music was composed and published for organists to play at that time. People who could not hear the prayer anyway listened to the organist. That practice should cease.

STRUCTURE

537. There are some variations, but the Eucharistic Prayers follow a basic structure: dialogue; preface; *Holy, Holy*; transition; institution narrative and consecration; memorial acclamation; anamnesis and offering; intercessions; final doxology.

Dialogue

538. Announcing their readiness to enter the great prayer, the priest and people engage in a dialogue (OM 31; GIRM 148). This dialogue begins the Eucharistic Prayer. All continue to stand, as they have since the in-

vitation to the prayer over the gifts. The dialogue is one of the parts of

the Mass recommended for singing (GIRM 40). The OM supplies notes 141
for this chant.

539. As the priest says, "The Lord be with you," he extends his hands
as he did for the greeting at the beginning of the Mass (OM 31; GIRM
148). The people respond. 202

540. As the priest invites everyone to lift their hearts, he raises his hands
(OM 31; GIRM 148). There is no other gesture in the Mass quite like this
one. It needs to be higher than the gesture used for the greeting, yet different from the one used for prayer. The people respond.

541. As the priest says, "Let us give thanks to the Lord our God," he
extends his hands (OM 31; GIRM 148). The description of this gesture is
the same as the one for the greeting, but many priests distinguish these
two extensions, as they do for the greeting at the beginning of Mass and
the collect. Thus a priest generally starts the dialogue by extending his 263
hands palms up toward the people as he greets them, lifts them palms
up for his next line, and moves them into the *orans* position for his last
line of dialogue.

Preface

542. In the name of the entire holy people, the priest proclaims the preface, a prayer of thanksgiving for God's work of salvation (GIRM 79a). The
preface expresses the reasons why the assembly gives thanks to God on
the occasion of its gathering. The Missal includes a series of prefaces for
seasons, feasts, and other occasions (OM 33–82). These variable prefaces
are especially appropriate for Eucharistic Prayers I and III. The selected
preface is usually marked with a ribbon before Mass begins to avoid a
delay while the priest searches for it. 85

543. At Masses with children the preface is one of the texts the priest
may change to find words more suited to children. He should take into
account the liturgical season (DMC 50). If the words are still difficult for
children to understand, "the text of prayers of the Roman Missal may be
adapted to the needs of children" in a way that preserves their purpose
and substance (DMC 51).

544. The priest prays the preface with his hands extended. He will probably maintain the gesture he made for the last line of the dialogue (OM
31; GIRM 148). 541

545. If the preface includes the names of the Trinity, Jesus, Mary, or the saint being honored in the Mass that day, the priest is to bow his head at the mention of the name (GIRM 275a), though not all priests do so.

546. The priest joins his hands at the conclusion of the preface (OM 31; GIRM 148).

547. If the priest is wearing a wireless microphone, switching it off after the preface will keep him from overpowering the voices of others making the next acclamation.

Holy, Holy

548. The entire assembly sings or says an acclamation of praise, the *Holy, Holy,* well known by its Latin title, the *Sanctus* (OM 31; GIRM 79b, 148). The Church on earth joins with the Church in heaven and with all creation to praise God. The GIRM does not explicitly recommend singing the Holy, Holy in Latin.

384, 622

549. It is not permitted to substitute another chant for the *Holy, Holy* (GIRM 366). However, at children's Masses the text of the *Holy, Holy* may be changed with permission of the competent authority. The text need not correspond exactly to the liturgical text (DMC 31). It should, however, respect the meaning of the original and its function in the rite (IOM 65).

550. In the United States the faithful kneel after the *Holy, Holy* (GIRM 43). The universal norms call for the entire assembly to remain standing until the consecration, but the custom is different in the United States.

844

551. There are exceptions to kneeling for the Eucharistic Prayer. People kneel "except when prevented on occasion by reasons of health, lack of space, the large number of people present, or some other good reason." The 2002 GIRM added "health" to the list; it would have been more precise to say "ill health." The universal paragraph 43 does not include the phrase "on occasion." That was added to the American norms, probably to end the practice of those communities standing throughout the Eucharistic Prayer, even though good reasons for standing remain.

576, 845

552. If incense will be used for the institution narrative (GIRM 150, 179, 276e, 277), the thurifer should probably take his or her position at this time. If there is more than one deacon, one of them places incense in the thurible (179), but any thurifer may do so. There is no provision for the

573

deacon or another minister to make the sign of the cross over the smoke as a priest does. Usually the thurifer then kneels on the front step of the sanctuary, facing the altar, holding the smoking thurible.

553. When the assembly kneels down, it will take a few moments. A good presider will wait until the kneelers have dropped, people are in position, and silence is restored before continuing the Eucharistic Prayer. If the priest has switched off a wireless microphone for the *Holy, Holy*, he turns it on again before resuming the prayer.

Transition: Prayer I from the Holy, Holy *to the Institution Narrative*

554. Eucharistic Prayer I continues after the *Holy, Holy* with a prayer asking God to bless the bread and wine (OM 84). The priest prays for leaders of the Church, including the current pope and the local bishop (GIRM 149). If there is a coadjutor or auxiliary bishop, he is also mentioned by *600* name. If there are several additional bishops, they are acknowledged with the collective formula "assistant Bishops" (GIRM 149).

555. The priest, whose hands were joined for the *Holy, Holy*, now extends them (OM 83). He is to bow his head at the name of Jesus in the first line of *546* this passage (GIRM 275a). He joins his hands briefly just before making the sign of the cross over the gifts of bread and wine, as he asks God to bless them. Then he extends his hands again as he prays for the Church.

556. The priest continues the prayer with a commemoration of the living (OM 85). He may mention some names aloud, though in practice most priests do not. He then allows the assembly a few moments to remember specifically those among the living for whom they wish to pray. He joins his hands during this short time and extends them again to continue the prayer.

557. The priest prays in communion with the saints (OM 86). The prayer mentions a number of saints from the Bible and from postapostolic times. *603* He is to bow his head at the names of Jesus and Mary and of the saint(s) honored at this Mass, if they are in the list (GIRM 275a), though few priests do. This prayer is extended with a few lines on days such as Christmas, Epiphany, the Easter Vigil, the octave of Easter, the Ascension, and Pentecost. On each of those days the prayer refers directly to the specific celebration that joins the Church of heaven with the Church on earth. The priest may join his hands for the doxology concluding this passage ("Through Christ our Lord. Amen.") Or he may omit this short text and its gesture. *524*

558. The priest asks God to accept the offering (OM 87). His hands remain extended for this prayer. On days such as Holy Thursday and at the Easter Vigil, this section of the prayer may be expanded to include a text that refers to the events being celebrated.

559. The priest extends his hands over the offerings while he asks God to bless and approve them (OM 88). He is not to make the sign of the cross a second time. He is to bow his head at the name of Jesus (GIRM 275a). The priest may join his hands for the doxology concluding this passage ("Through Christ our Lord. Amen.") Or he may omit this short text and its gesture.

524

Transition: Other Eucharistic Prayers from the Holy, Holy to the Institution Narrative

560. After the *Holy, Holy* the other Eucharistic Prayers continue with the thanksgiving begun in the preface (OM 100, 108, 117; GIRM 79a). The length of this text varies considerably among the Eucharistic Prayers.

561. The priest extends his hands over the offerings and prays for the coming of the Holy Spirit (OM 101, 109, 118), that the gifts may become Christ's Body and Blood, and that they may bring salvation to those who partake of them (GIRM 79c). This part of the Eucharistic Prayer is called the epiclesis. The Eastern Rites, but not the Roman Rite, consider the epiclesis the consecration. There is no explicit epiclesis in Eucharistic Prayer I.

599
565

562. The priest makes the sign of the cross over the offerings while proclaiming the epiclesis, bows his head at the name of Jesus (GIRM 275a), and rejoins his hands. The OM points out that he makes the sign of the cross once. This should be understood, but in the pre-Vatican II Missal the priest made multiple signs of the cross over the elements prior to the institution narrative.

563. The deacon is to kneel at the epiclesis (GIRM 179). This rubric was inserted into the 2000 GIRM from CB 155. In the universal document (not in the American edition), the people kneel at this time as well. The intention of this insertion is clear, but some implications are not. In Eucharistic Prayer I there is no epiclesis, but presumably the deacon kneels when the priest extends his hands over the offerings (OM 88). GIRM 179 also says the deacon may assist the priest with the Missal as needed, but this will be difficult from his knees. The American edition of the GIRM has the people kneeling after the *Holy, Holy*, the deacon kneeling at the

550, 669

559

epiclesis, and the priest not kneeling at all. It is perhaps an oversight that the deacon takes a posture different from that of the priest and the people in the United States. Some bishops have excused infirm deacons from kneeling.

564. A server may ring a bell "a little before the consecration, when appropriate" (GIRM 150). Traditionally this happened when the priest extended his hands over the gifts, but the GIRM does not say precisely when it may happen. Before Vatican II the bell signaled the faithful that the consecration was near. Now that Mass is in the vernacular and the priest is facing the people and speaking in a clear voice, the need for the bell has vanished. The IOM omits the expression "when appropriate," as if to imply that this bell is not optional (118). But it is.

157, 572, 582

Institution Narrative and Consecration

565. In the heart of the Eucharistic Prayer, the priest tells the story of the Last Supper (OM 89–90, 102–103, 110–111, 119–120). This section is known as the "institution narrative" and in the Roman Rite is called the "consecration" (GIRM 79d).

561

566. The priest is to pronounce the words of this section distinctly and clearly (OM 89, 102, 110, 119) because of the Western tradition that these are the words of consecration. This instruction applies to the entire institution narrative, not just to the quotations of the words of Jesus. Of course, the entire prayer should be pronounced distinctly and clearly.

567. The priest picks up the bread as he begins the narrative (OM 89, 102, 110, 119). In practice, the priest picks up one large host or one loaf. If there are many hosts, he need not hold them all. He is not to raise the paten.

579

568. Eucharistic Prayer I calls for the priest to raise his eyes (OM 89). Luke says Jesus looked up to heaven for the miracle of the loaves (9:16), and John says he raised his eyes for prayer at the Last Supper (17:1), but the Gospels say nothing about Jesus' gaze when he took up bread at the Last Supper. The other Eucharistic Prayers do not call for the priest to raise his eyes, possibly to avoid overdramatizing the institution narrative.

569. As he quotes the words of Jesus, "the priest bows slightly" (GIRM 275b). This is not as deep a bow as the profound bow made at other times of the Mass. The institution narrative is the only instance where the rubrics call for a slight bow. It probably intends to help the priest show reverence and focus his attention. But he is not speaking to the host.

580

He may need to adjust the volume of his voice if this posture brings the wireless microphone closer to his mouth.

570. The priest is not to break the bread when he tells of Jesus performing the same action (RS 55). Some priests started doing this, probably because they saw it as a natural extension of taking bread as Jesus did. But the Mass is not a dramatic representation of the Last Supper. It is a sacramental celebration of the Eucharist. The overarching structure of the Mass has a place for the breaking of the bread. It follows the time of giving thanks, just as it did at the Last Supper. First the priest finishes the prayer of thanksgiving, the Eucharistic Prayer. Then he moves on to the Communion rite, which will include the breaking of the bread.

647

571. The priest shows the consecrated bread to the people (OM 89, 102, 110, 119). He shows the bread; he need not lift it high in elevation. Even before the Council the priest was only instructed to show the bread, not to elevate it. But with his back to the people, the only way he could show it was to elevate it. Today the bread need not be lifted so high. By choosing a medium position for the elements, the priest reserves their elevation for the conclusion of the Eucharistic Prayer.

581

606

572. A server may ring a bell as the priest shows the bread (GIRM 150). It is optional. In the past the bell was important to alert the faithful—especially the great many who would not be sharing Communion weekly—that they could now adore Christ present in the consecrated host. Now that the priest faces the people and speaks the Eucharistic Prayer clearly in the vernacular, and now that the highlight of the Mass is the Communion of the faithful, the former need for the bell has vanished.

564, 582

573. Incense may be swung when the priest shows the consecrated bread (GIRM 150, 179, 276e). The thurifer may be a deacon, acolyte, server, or another minister. The thurifer, who kneels with the rest of the assembly, bows to the consecrated bread, swings the thurible three times, and bows again (277).

583

552

574. Many people in the assembly bow their heads while the priest shows them the consecrated bread. This devotional practice intends to show respect for the Eucharist. The OM and GIRM do not mention it. This practice means well, but it defeats the purpose of the action. The priest shows the bread to the people. The implied rubric is that people should look at it.

584

575. Some people strike their breast and say, "My Lord and my God," as Thomas said when Jesus appeared to him after the resurrection (John

585

20:28). These devotional practices have never been part of the rubrics of the Mass. They are not forbidden; they are not required; they manifest popular piety. Consequently, it would not be appropriate for people to say this text aloud or for the deacon visibly to strike his breast as if the liturgy expected everyone to imitate him.

576. After showing the consecrated bread, the priest places it back on the paten and genuflects in adoration (OM 89, 102, 110, 119; GIRM 274). This is the first of three genuflections the priest makes during the course of the Mass. A genuflection is made by bending the right knee to the ground (GIRM 274). In practice, many priests place their hands on the altar table to steady themselves. Some priests who are too infirm to genuflect make a profound bow instead. If members of the faithful are standing for the Eucharistic Prayer, they make a profound bow while the priest genuflects (GIRM 43). This is the same gesture they made during the Creed. *586, 674* *52, 171* *551, 843* *383*

577. If those who are kneeling wish to make an additional sign of reverence, it would be more appropriate for them to bow their heads while the priest genuflects than to do so while he shows them the elements. *574*

578. In the pre-Vatican II Missal the priest removed the pall before picking up the chalice. The GIRM and OM are silent about this. In practice, many priests exercise the option not to use the pall at all. However, the GIRM permits the priest to cover the chalice with the pall during the preparation of the gifts, after it is set on the altar (142). If this happened, the priest should remove the pall before picking up the chalice during the institution narrative. *109, 480*

579. The priest picks up the chalice and holds it a little above the altar as he tells of Jesus taking the cup (OM 90, 103, 111, 120). If more than one chalice rests on the altar, he picks up only one. *567*

580. The priest bows slightly as he quotes the words of Jesus (OM). He repeats the posture he takes when quoting the words of Jesus over the bread. He does not speak into the chalice. He may need to adjust the volume of his voice if this posture brings the wireless microphone closer to his mouth. *569*

581. The priest shows the chalice to the people (OM 90, 103, 111, 120). He need not lift it high in elevation. By choosing a medium position for showing the elements, the priest reserves their elevation for the conclusion of the Eucharistic Prayer. *571* *606*

582. A server may ring a bell as the priest shows the chalice (GIRM 150). It is optional. For symmetry, if the bell is omitted for one of the elements, it should be omitted for both.

564, 572

583. Incense may be swung when the priest shows the chalice (GIRM 150, 179, 276e). The thurifer bows to the chalice, swings the thurible three times, and bows again (277).

573

584. Many people in the assembly bow their heads while the priest shows them the chalice. The implied rubric, though, is that people look at the chalice as the priest shows it to them.

574

585. Some strike their breast and say, "My Lord and my God." These devotions are not forbidden and are not required; they manifest popular piety. It would not be appropriate for people to say this text aloud or for the deacon visibly to strike his breast, as if the liturgy expected everyone to imitate him.

575

586. After showing the chalice, the priest replaces it on the corporal and genuflects in adoration (OM 90, 103, 111, 120; GIRM 274). This is the second of three genuflections he makes during the course of the Mass. If members of the faithful are standing for the Eucharistic Prayer, they make a profound bow while the priest genuflects (GIRM 43). In the pre-Vatican II Missal the priest then covered the chalice with the pall. The use of the pall is optional. The Missal's elimination of many references to it seems to discourage its use.

576, 674

551

109

587. If those who are kneeling wish to make an additional sign of reverence, it would be more appropriate for them to bow their heads while the priest genuflects than to do so while he shows them the elements.

584

588. Outside the United States the universal GIRM asks the assembly to change its posture from kneeling to standing after the consecration (43).

616

Memorial Acclamation

589. The priest announces the moment for all to proclaim the mystery of faith, and the people respond with an acclamation (OM 91, 104, 112, 121; GIRM 151). In some places the deacon makes this announcement, but it belongs to the priest. The post-Vatican II Sacramentary in English had the priest make the acclamation along with the people, but the universal OM had always assigned it to the people alone.

590. The Missal provides a choice of acclamations. The Latin Missal provided three choices; the postconciliar English Sacramentary offered

four. The USCCB debated the retention of "Christ has died" in the revised English translation of the Missal because it is not a direct translation of any of the Latin acclamations. Still more acclamations are supplied in the Eucharistic Prayers for Masses with children. Other chants are not to be substituted (GIRM 366). In practice, many parishes repeat the same acclamation throughout a liturgical season, but there are no rules governing the choice at any particular Mass.

591. Singing is encouraged at Mass, especially the dialogues of the priest and the people (GIRM 40). The singing of this acclamation is so strongly *141* encouraged that the OM provides musical notation for the priest and for the people's first option. The instrumental introduction often signals which acclamation is being sung; otherwise the cantor needs to start it. When the acclamation is spoken, the priest generally starts it, but anyone may do so, especially since the rubrics assign the acclamation to the people, not to the priest.

Anamnesis and Offering

592. In the anamnesis the Church recalls especially the death, resurrection, and ascension of Christ (GIRM 79e). It is the first text spoken by the priest alone as he resumes the Eucharistic Prayer. He extends his hands (OM 92, 105, 113, 122).

593. The priest states this memorial immediately after the acclamation (OM 92, 105, 113, 122), even though everyone has just sung a very similar text. The acclamation is also an anamnesis, and the priest's words are *589* somewhat redundant.

594. In the offering (OM 93–94, 105, 113, 122) the Church gathered at this Eucharist "offers in the Holy Spirit the spotless Victim to the Father" (GIRM 79f). In this action the faithful "also learn to offer themselves" to deepen their unity with God and with one another.

595. Because of the significance of this offering, it should not be confused with the preparation of the altar or with the offertory chant. Earlier in the Mass the gifts were brought forward for their preparation, not as an offering. This is when the offering takes place. *448, 839*

596. In Eucharistic Prayer I the priest performs additional gestures (OM 94). As he prays for God's angel to carry these gifts to the heavenly altar, he joins his hands and bows, then stands up straight and signs himself with the cross. The OM just calls this a bow, such as the one in the Creed, *383*

but the GIRM lists both of these among the profound bows (275b). If the priest concludes the prayer with the optional doxology, he joins his hands for it.

597. In the third Eucharistic Prayer for children and the first for Masses of reconciliation, the offering includes a reference to the name of Jesus. The priest is to bow his head (GIRM 275a); in practice, many priests do not.

Intercessions

598. In the intercessions, prayers are made for the members of the Church, the living and the dead (OM 95–97, 105, 113, 122; GIRM 79g).

599. Except for Eucharistic Prayer I, the intercessions begin with a second epiclesis. In this case the priest calls on the Holy Spirit to come upon *561* the assembly of those sharing this Eucharist. The pairing of this with the previous epiclesis would have been more explicit if the rubrics had called for the priest to extend his hands over the assembled faithful for this appeal.

600. Prayer is made for the current pope and the local bishop. In Eucharistic Prayer I they are mentioned earlier. If there is a coadjutor or auxiliary *554* bishop, he is also mentioned by name. If there are several additional bishops, they are acknowledged with the collective formula "assistant Bishops" (GIRM 149).

601. Wherever the intercessions mention Jesus, Mary, or the saint in whose honor Mass is celebrated, the priest is to bow his head (GIRM 275a), though not all priests do so.

602. In Eucharistic Prayer I the priest invites the people to pray for the dead. He may mention some names aloud. Then he joins his hands and observes a few moments of silence. He extends his hands again as he resumes the prayer (OM 96). If he says the short doxology concluding this section, he joins his hands again.

524 603. In Eucharistic Prayer I, when the priest acknowledges the sinfulness of the gathered faithful, he strikes his breast (OM 96). This is the same gesture made by the entire assembly when they pray the *Confiteor* during the act of penitence (OM 4). He extends his hands as he continues *216* to pray for the intercession of a second group of saints. Those named in *557* this group are some of the early apostles and martyrs, primarily from the Church of Rome. If one is the saint in whose honor Mass is celebrated, the priest is to bow his head at the mention of his or her name (GIRM

275a). The priest joins his hands for the brief doxology that precedes the final doxology of the Eucharistic Prayer. In this case the brief doxology is not optional. If the priest says this too definitively, some people may answer "Amen" when they should not. It will help if the presider moves from these words directly into the final doxology.

524

Final Doxology

604. The Eucharistic Prayer concludes as the priest glorifies God in a final doxology, and the people confirm and conclude it with their great "Amen" (OM 98, 106, 114, 123; GIRM 79h).

605. There is no reference to the pall in the rubrics of the doxology. In the past the priest had re-covered the chalice with the pall after the institution narrative and uncovered it again before the elevation. The pall is optional, but if it is being used, it should not be elevated with the chalice.

109, 586

606. The priest picks up the paten with the consecrated bread as well as the chalice (OM 98, 106, 114, 123; GIRM 151). If there is a deacon, he stands next to the priest and holds the chalice while the priest takes up the paten (GIRM 180). The *vessels* are to be elevated; the priest is not to lift one host. Compared with the other occasions when the bread and wine are held up, this lifting of the vessels should have the greatest height. During the preparation of the gifts, the priest holds the bread and wine a little above the altar. During the institution narrative he shows the elements to the people, but here, at the end of the Eucharistic Prayer, the paten and the chalice are elevated.

438

461, 475

571, 581

607. No more than two vessels need to be lifted. Sometimes the clergy try to hold more than they can handle.

608. In the pre–Vatican II practice the priest lifted the host (not the paten) in one hand above the chalice in his other hand. By lifting an entire vessel of consecrated bread, the priest now manifests more completely the reason for giving glory to God.

609. The paten and chalice may be lifted side by side. The host no longer needs to be raised higher than the chalice. Both elements are being elevated in the doxology. Whether the deacon lifts the chalice or the priest lifts both vessels, the paten and chalice may be held at equal heights.

610. The singing of dialogues is encouraged (GIRM 40). The OM provides notes for the final doxology right on the page with the text for each

141

Eucharistic Prayer (98, 106, 114, 123), and an alternative version of the chant appears in the Missal's first appendix. Other versions may be used.

611. The priest sings or says the doxology alone. The people sing or say the Amen (GIRM 151, 236). After the Council the significance of the Amen concluding the Eucharistic Prayer became clearer. Prior to the 1960s it seemed to be just one more of many Amens. Some parishes, in an effort to underline the significance of the conclusion to the Eucharistic Prayer, invited everyone to proclaim the entire doxology together with the priest. But the rubrics have always assigned the body of the doxology to the priest alone.

612. The priest is to bow his head at the names of the Trinity (GIRM 275a) in the doxology. This is difficult to do while elevating the vessels.

613. The people acclaim "Amen." The response is assigned to the people, but the priest usually sings along. In 1972 the Bishops' Committee on the Liturgy (United States Catholic Conference) wrote, "To be most effective, the Amen may be repeated or augmented" (Music in Catholic Worship, 58). The Committee on the Liturgy reaffirmed this position in 1996 (*Committee on the Liturgy Newsletter* 33 [January/February 1997] 5). After the Amen the priest—with the deacon if there is one—places the vessels on the corporal again (OM 124; GIRM 151, 180). Some clergy tire out and lower the vessels while the people are still singing, but the song and gesture should go together.

COMMUNION RITE

614. In the Communion rite the Body and Blood of Christ are "received as spiritual food by the faithful" (GIRM 80). They have prepared themselves through the introductory rites and the Liturgy of the Word. The bread and wine have been readied. The priest has led the people in the Eucharistic Prayer, in which the Holy Spirit has transformed the bread and wine into the Body and Blood of Christ. Now everyone shares the sacrament of salvation.

LORD'S PRAYER

615. The faithful, who will shortly be sharing Communion, pray together in the words Jesus gave his disciples. The Lord's Prayer begins with an introduction by the priest and concludes with an embolism and doxology (GIRM 81).

616. In the United States everyone stands after the great "Amen" and before the priest introduces the Lord's Prayer. In the original universal GIRM, everyone has been standing since the memorial acclamation, and they simply retain their posture (43).

588, 843

617. The priest invites the people to pray the Lord's Prayer (OM 124; GIRM 152). He does so with his hands joined. He uses the same gesture when inviting people to pray at other times of the Mass and while greeting them before the gospel. In a way it feels more natural to open one's hands when addressing the assembly, but the GIRM does not nuance different extensions of hands as it does bows. The gesture used when addressing the people differs from the one addressing God in the prayer.

255, 345, 388, 786

618. After the Council the Sacramentary included four English versions of the text for the priest to introduce the Lord's Prayer. It seemed to imply that he was free to use these or similar words, and that became widely practiced. The Latin original had only supplied one text, which was retained as the only one in the 2002 OM (124). The USCCB requested that four alternate introductions be retained in the English translation of the Missal. At children's Masses the priest is encouraged to use his own words when introducing the Lord's Prayer (DMC 23).

619. The priest and people pray the Lord's Prayer together, as disciples of Jesus, who binds them together under a common Father (OM 124; GIRM 152).

620. The priest extends his hands for the prayer (OM 124; GIRM 152), as he does for other presidential prayers of the Mass.

263, 508, 544, 788

621. No gesture is recommended for the assembly. In practice, some of the faithful join hands, probably to signify their unity as they pray in the first-person plural. Others lift their hands as the priest does. But there is no instruction for the people's hands in the OM or the GIRM. In 1975 the Congregation for Divine Worship did not forbid the holding of hands: "The prolonged holding of hands is of itself a sign of communion. . . . Further, it is a liturgical gesture introduced spontaneously but on personal initiative; it is not in the rubrics" (*Notitiae* 11 [1975] 226). It would be excessive for the priest to invite this gesture; nothing should overshadow the symbol of unity in the Communion of the faithful.

622. The singing of the Lord's Prayer is encouraged (GIRM 40). The OM includes notes for singing the introduction, prayer, embolism, and doxology (124–125), and two other versions appear in the Missal's first

141

appendix. This is one of the texts that the GIRM recommends people learn to sing in Latin (41), but few assemblies have mastered it.

623. In the embolism the priest expands the prayer with a petition for freedom from evil and sin (OM 125; GIRM 153). He keeps his hands extended.

624. The people conclude the prayer with an acclamation (OM 125; GIRM 153). The priest joins his hands for this text. Although many priests make this acclamation with the people, it is designed to be the people's response. The priest is to remain silent for it. The acclamation is based on a line that Christians of other ecclesial communities use to conclude the Lord's Prayer, but the Catholic tradition does not. The earliest manuscripts of Matthew's Gospel do not include this acclamation with the prayer Jesus taught his disciples, but it appeared in a Church document by the end of the first century (the *Didache*) and found its way into later Bibles and worship practices.

RITE OF PEACE

625. In the rite of peace the Church prays for peace, and the faithful express it to one another (GIRM 82).

626. At Masses with children the entire rite of peace is not listed among the parts that should always be included in the Communion rite (DMC 53). In the interests of brevity and simplicity, it could be omitted for the sake of the children. Most children, however, grasp its meaning and enter its ritual elements.

Prayer to Christ

627. The priest alone offers a prayer to Christ for the peace and unity of the Church (OM 126; GIRM 154). He extends his hands for the prayer. He is to bow his head at the name of Jesus (GIRM 275a). All answer "Amen" to the priest's prayer (OM 126).

628. Singing is encouraged for dialogues between the priest and the people (GIRM 40). The OM provides notes on the page for singing this prayer and its conclusion.

Greeting of Peace

629. The priest wishes the Lord's peace to the people, and they respond (OM 127; GIRM 154).

630. The priest faces the people for this greeting (OM 127; GIRM 154). In most churches he is already facing them, because the altar is apart from the wall, in accordance with GIRM 299. This rubric should not be necessary. *67*

631. The priest extends and then joins his hands to wish everyone peace. *202, 503,* It is a gesture similar to the one he uses for greeting the people and when *539, 786,* inviting them to pray during the preparation of the gifts. *802*

632. The singing of dialogues is encouraged (GIRM 40). Notes appear *141* on the page of the Missal for this exchange (OM 127).

Sign of Peace

633. The priest invites the people to exchange peace with one another (OM 128; GIRM 154). If there is a deacon, he speaks the cue (GIRM 181).

634. Singing is encouraged (GIRM 40). The OM supplies notes for chant- *141* ing the invitation to the sign of peace, though this is rarely done.

635. A deacon is to face the people and keep his hands joined. If the altar is apart from the wall, in accordance with GIRM 299, the deacon is already facing the people, so this rubric is unnecessary. The deacon *67* is to keep his hands joined, as he does when greeting the people before proclaiming the gospel and giving the dismissal. The priest will also *345, 814* have just joined his hands after the greeting of peace. *631*

636. At Masses with children the priest is encouraged to use his own words for this invitation (DMC 23). Logically, the same would be true of a deacon. Neither the GIRM nor the OM indicates that this invitation is given "in these or similar words," but it often is. The IOM cautions against using an explanatory commentary (129).

637. The sign of peace is given "when appropriate" (OM 128; GIRM 154, 181). Other sections of the GIRM, though, imply that the peace will be given (82, 239). The first Christians exchanged peace at the Eucharist, but the tradition fell into disuse until after the Second Vatican Council. It returned as an option, perhaps in fear that people who resisted increased participation at Mass would find the sign of peace too much to bear. Over the years this sign has become an important part of worship for many Catholics. As the OM points out in a rare interpretation of a ritual action it describes, this ritual exchange symbolizes peace, communion, and charity. If that is the purpose of the sign of peace, it is hard to imagine when it would not be "appropriate."

638. If the priest is wearing a wireless microphone, he switches it off to avoid broadcasting the words he speaks to individuals.

639. The priest gives peace to the deacon or another minister (OM 128). In a rubric new to the 2002 GIRM, the priest is not to leave the sanctuary when sharing peace with others (154). In the United States, though, "for a good reason, on special occasions (for example, in the case of a funeral, a wedding, or when civic leaders are present) the priest may offer the sign of peace to a few of the faithful near the sanctuary" (154).

848

640. The deacon receives peace from the priest and offers it to other ministers (GIRM 181). The former English translation of this sentence said the deacon may offer peace "to other ministers near him" (pre-2002 GIRM 136). The 2002 GIRM now says more literally that he "may offer it to those other ministers who are closer to him," implying that the deacon will give peace to those near the deacon, and the priest will give peace to those near the priest. In practice, the exchange of peace is given with fewer restrictions.

641. The faithful are to offer peace "only to those who are nearest and in a sober manner" (GIRM 82). Also new to the 2002 GIRM is a text suggested to the people. Each is encouraged to say, "The peace of the Lord be with you always," and the recommended response is "Amen" (154). This response, given to another layperson, is markedly different from the one the assembly has just made to the priest. In practice, most people say, "Peace be with you," or they improvise another greeting. The same greeting is often given as a response. Virtually no one answers "Amen."

629, 849

642. As to the sign, it should not overshadow the sign of unity coming in Communion. Most people exchange a handshake. Some embrace. Some kiss. Some nod the head. Some wave at someone a short distance away. People usually exchange peace courteously and sincerely.

643. Some parishes developed a custom of singing an explanatory song during this time. The OM and GIRM do not envision this at all. The point of the ritual is to involve everyone in wishing and receiving signs of peace. It is not an ideal time to ask the assembly or even a choir or cantor to sing. "The sign itself is sufficiently strong and expressive and does not need explanatory song" (IOM 129).

644. In some parishes extraordinary ministers of Holy Communion enter the sanctuary during the sign of peace. But they do not approach the altar until after the Communion of the priest. This further restricts those with whom the priest shares peace.

667, 713

645. There should be a clear distinction between the sign of peace and the breaking of the bread. The actions and texts that pertain to the breaking of the bread should not encroach on the time the assembly is exchanging its peace.

658

BREAKING BREAD

646. Jesus broke bread at the feeding of the multitude, at the Last Supper, and at post-resurrection meals with his disciples. The Acts of the Apostles refers to the Eucharist as "the breaking of the bread." "Just as many grains of wheat are ground, kneaded, and baked together to become one loaf, which is then broken and shared out among many to bring them into one table-fellowship, so those gathered are made one body in the one bread of life that is Christ (see 1 Cor 10:17)" (IOM 130).

Fraction

647. The priest breaks the bread over the paten (OM 129; GIRM 83, 155). He may also break it over whatever larger vessel is holding the consecrated bread for the entire assembly (GIRM 331; IOM 51). This rite is also called the "fraction."

100
570

648. Only priests and deacons may break the consecrated bread (GIRM 83, 240). By limiting the breaking of bread to the priest and deacon alone, the legislation makes it harder for parishes to honor the GIRM's preference that bread resemble food (321). The sign of the bread is more deeply conveyed if everyone receives a piece of broken bread, but by limiting the number of ministers for the ritual breaking, the GIRM reinforces the use of unbroken bread in the form of independently baked hosts in order to save time.

428, 856

649. Also new to the 2002 GIRM is the preference that the breaking of bread "should not be unnecessarily prolonged, nor should it be accorded undue importance" (83). It is hard to reconcile this statement with others in the same paragraph: the *Lamb of God* "may be repeated as many times as necessary until the rite has reached its conclusion," and the breaking of the bread "gave the entire Eucharistic Action its name in apostolic times." The breaking of bread must have seemed important to the apostles (321).

661

650. During the fraction additional Communion vessels may be brought to the altar (NDR 37). The documents never say who brings them. The deacon or servers bring vessels to the altar at the preparation of the gifts.

419, 753

Logically, the deacon or servers would bring the additional vessels to the altar for the Communion rite. Extraordinary ministers of Communion approach the altar later, after the priest receives, so if they bring vessels forward at this point, they withdraw from the altar afterward.

713

651. Many priests have their next lines memorized. If so, it would be appropriate for the server or another minister to remove the Missal from the altar at this time. There is no need for it to remain on the altar for the distribution of Communion. If a bookstand was used to support the Missal, it also would be removed.

420, 718

652. Once the additional vessels are in place, the priest breaks and divides the bread into them (NDR 37). A deacon may assist. This distribution of the Eucharistic bread into vessels at Mass is reserved to deacons and priests. This seems unusual, because outside of Mass lay ministers perform similar actions when they take a consecrated host from a ciborium in the tabernacle and place it in a pyx for Communion to the sick.

653. The priest is to break the bread "into parts for distribution to at least some of the faithful" (321). Some priests use a host about two and a half inches in diameter, break it at this time, but consume all its parts at Communion. It seems like a small matter, but it violates the symbol that this part of the Mass strives to create. Even a host that size should be shared with other communicants. "One of these portions is consumed by the priest, while the rest are distributed to at least a few others" (IOM 131). The breaking of bread "will bring out more clearly the force and importance of the sign of unity of all in the one bread, and of the sign of charity by the fact that the one bread is distributed among the brothers and sisters" (GIRM 321). Larger hosts or loaves would be even more appropriate.

676, 691

435

654. The priest puts a particle of consecrated bread into the chalice (OM 129; GIRM 155). This signifies "the unity of the Body and Blood of the Lord in the work of salvation, namely of the living and glorious Body of Jesus Christ" (GIRM 83). This rite is sometimes called the "commingling."

676, 698

655. While he places the particle in the chalice, the priest offers a prayer for the eternal life of all who share Communion (OM 129; GIRM 155). The priest is to recite these words quietly. It is not precisely one of the texts "he prays only in his own name, asking that he may exercise his ministry with greater attention and devotion" (GIRM 33), but it is not meant to be said aloud nor to evoke an "Amen" from the congregation.

656. The use of the pall is optional (GIRM 142, 118c), but if the priest re-covered the chalice with it after the Amen that concludes the doxology, he needs to remove it for the commingling. The OM and GIRM make no reference to the pall at this time.

109, 605

Lamb of God

657. While the bread is broken, the *Lamb of God* is sung or said (OM 130; GIRM 83, 155). The breaking of bread reminds the community of the Passover lamb, slaughtered for the salvation of God's chosen people. All pray for mercy and peace.

658. The *Lamb of God* begins with the breaking of the bread (OM 130; GIRM 83, 155). It should not be anticipated while the sign of peace is still being exchanged.

645

659. The singing of the *Lamb of God* is encouraged (GIRM 40), and the OM supplies notes for the chant (130). Other melodies are found in the *Graduale Romanum*. The GIRM says this litany should be led by the can-tor or choir with the people responding (83, 155), but in practice many congregations sing the entire text. The GIRM does not explicitly recom-mend singing the *Lamb of God* in Latin.

141

384, 622

660. The documents do not say who starts the *Lamb of God*. If it is sung, a cantor, choir, or the entire assembly usually begins. If it is recited, the priest usually begins. But even when it is recited, it could be started by a deacon, cantor, commentator, or the entire assembly upon the cue of the breaking of bread. If the priest is wearing a wireless microphone and if the *Lamb of God* is sung by everyone, he keeps it off to avoid overpower-ing the people. If he leads the *Lamb of God*, he switches it on.

661. If the breaking of bread takes time, the petitions of the *Lamb of God* may be repeated to cover the action (OM 130; GIRM 83). This rubric im-plies the use of a loaf of bread or several large hosts that will be broken into pieces in an action that will take some time. No matter how many times the first petition is repeated, the last petition always concludes with "grant us peace."

435, 649

662. The text of the *Lamb of God* should not be substituted with another chant (GIRM 366), but at Masses with children "it is permissible to use with the melodies appropriate vernacular texts, accepted by competent authority, even if these do not correspond exactly to the liturgical texts"

(DMC 31). Some musical settings of the *Lamb of God* amplify the text with a wider range of Christological titles or descriptive clauses. This custom fits within the tradition of Catholic litanies and preserves the original text of the *Lamb of God* while expanding the range of its praise. Speaking of the *Lamb of God* in 1982, the United States Catholic Conference wrote, "One should not hesitate to add tropes to the litany so that the prayerfulness of the rite may be enriched" (Liturgical Music Today, 20). The NCCB's Committee on the Liturgy reaffirmed this position in 1996 (*Committee on the Liturgy Newsletter* 33 [January/February 1997] 5), and it has approved the publication of musical settings with these additions.

Communion from the Tabernacle

663. Everyone should receive Communion from the bread and wine brought to the altar at the Mass they attend. The Communion they receive is not just heavenly bread from a remote source; it is the Body and Blood of Christ consecrated from the bread and wine the people brought as symbols of themselves. At Mass, "the memorial sacrifice of his Body and Blood is offered to the Father; and the Holy Spirit is invoked to sanctify the gifts and transform those who partake of them into the Body of Christ" (IOM 112). "It is preferable that the faithful be able to receive hosts consecrated in the same Mass" (RS 89). "It is most desirable that the faithful, just as the priest himself is bound to do, receive the Lord's Body from hosts consecrated at the same Mass . . . so that even by means of the signs Communion will stand out more clearly as a participation in
437 the sacrifice actually being celebrated" (GIRM 85).

664. Many Catholic parishes violate this principle at almost every Mass. A Communion minister goes to the tabernacle, brings a ciborium of previously consecrated hosts to the altar, where they are distributed unawares to many of the faithful in attendance. Everyone receives Communion, but not everyone participates in the sacrifice by means of the signs. A careful preparation for Mass will set out enough bread for the entire assembly
115 (GIRM 85, 118c).

665. Circumstances may call for the use of hosts from the tabernacle, "for example, the late arrival of unexpected numbers." But "the faithful are not ordinarily to be given Holy Communion from the tabernacle with hosts consecrated at a previous Mass" (IOM 131). The GIRM finds the idea so outside the spirit of the Mass that it never gives directions for how this might be done.

666. In the rare instance when they are needed, "these hosts may be brought reverently but without ceremony from the tabernacle to the altar at the breaking of the bread" (IOM 131). It would not be appropriate for candle bearers to accompany this procession.

667. It is common to see a Communion minister bring the hosts to the altar, but the IOM envisions that the priest or deacon brings them, probably because Communion ministers are not to approach the altar until after the priest has received Communion. "If it is necessary to use the hosts consecrated from a previous Mass, a priest or deacon should bring the reserved sacrament to the altar from the tabernacle, reverently but without ceremony" (121). But this seems a needless inconvenience, especially if the tabernacle is located in a separate chapel apart from the sanctuary (GIRM 315). 644, 713

128, 762

Posture

668. After the *Lamb of God* the faithful in the United States kneel, unless the diocesan bishop determines otherwise (GIRM 43). This has been a custom in the United States for some time, but it was never part of the legislation until the 2002 GIRM.

669. In the universal GIRM everyone remains standing after the *Lamb of God*. There is nothing in the Mass to indicate that this is an appropriate time to kneel. In the universal GIRM the faithful kneel during the institution narrative as a devotional practice during the consecration, but the universal practice never calls for the entire assembly to kneel at any other time. The Communion rite retains more unanimity if the faithful maintain the same posture throughout, in union with the priest and deacon. The singing at Communion will also be enhanced if all stand. It would be praiseworthy for a diocesan bishop to determine the appropriateness of having the faithful remain standing after the *Lamb of God*. 563

704, 749

722

THE PRIEST'S COMMUNION

Preparation

670. The priest prepares for Communion by reciting a prayer quietly (OM 131; GIRM 84, 156). The Missal offers two possible texts. The first asks Jesus to free the priest from his sins, keep him faithful, and never let him be separated from Christ. The second asks Jesus that the result of this Communion be not condemnation but strengthening and health.

The priest offers one, not both of these prayers. It is noteworthy that both are addressed to Jesus Christ.

671. These are among the prayers recited quietly by the priest, that he might exercise his ministry with greater devotion (GIRM 33). Consequently, he may recite his prayer of preparation during the *Lamb of God*.

672. The priest joins his hands for this prayer (OM 131). This is not a public oration such as one of the presidential prayers, which call for him to pray with hands extended. He is to bow his head at the name of Jesus (GIRM 275a).

673. The faithful should also pray silently to prepare themselves in a similar way for Communion (GIRM 84). Communion is an action of the whole Body of Christ, but each one prepares individually as well as in common.

"Behold the Lamb of God"

674. The priest genuflects (OM 132; GIRM 157), the third time during
the course of the Mass that he does so.

675. The priest picks up some of the bread consecrated at the same Mass and holds it up over the paten or over the chalice (OM 132; GIRM 84, 157). Prior to the 2002 Missal, the priest was to hold this bread over the paten. The option for holding up the chalice is new, although it was widely practiced even before the revised Missal. Catholics believe that Christ is truly present under both forms of Communion, and the GIRM promotes the Communion of the faithful under both these forms (281). Holding up the chalice together with the consecrated bread is a stronger symbol of Communion.

676. In practice, some priests reassemble the remaining parts of the broken host and hold it up as if nothing had happened to it. Having split the host in half and then broken a particle into the chalice, they hold the two remaining parts together and conceal the missing area with their fingers. The host should have been broken into more pieces for distribution to
the faithful. People do not need to see an unbroken host at this time. The gesture is not called for, and it minimizes the significance of the breaking of the bread.

677. Some priests lift the entire vessel of bread in one hand and the chalice in the other. The rubrics call for him to hold a host, not the vessel, and to consume it without ever setting it down. Lifting the vessel has the advan-

tage of showing both elements equally in the vessels from which the entire community will share Communion. Lifting only the elements the priest will receive focuses this action on its personal and hieratic significance.

678. The priest is to face the people (OM 132; GIRM 157). This rubric is a holdover from the days when the priest said Mass with his back to the people. The GIRM calls for a freestanding altar at which the priest stands facing the people throughout the Communion rite (299). 67

679. If people in the United States are still changing postures from standing to kneeling, it would be courteous for the priest to wait until they are ready before beginning his text.

680. If the priest is wearing a wireless microphone, and if he has had it off for the sign of peace and the *Lamb of God*, he switches it on for his text.

681. The priest, quoting words of John the Baptist (John 1:35) and holding the Eucharistic elements, acknowledges Jesus as the Lamb of God and proclaims those blessed who come to the table (OM 132; GIRM 84, 157).

682. At Masses with children the priest is encouraged to use his own words for the invitation to Communion (DMC 23).

683. The people respond, expressing their unworthiness by quoting the centurion who said to Jesus: "Lord, I am not worthy" (Matthew 8:8; Luke 7:6-7). The priest makes this response together with the people (OM 132; GIRM 84, 157).

684. The people say their text once (OM 132). This rubric first appeared immediately after the Council because the pre-Vatican II Missal had people make this response three times. The reminder to do it once should no longer be necessary.

685. Singing is encouraged for dialogues between priest and people (GIRM 40). The first appendix of the Missal suggests musical notation *141* for chanting this invitation and response. *693, 702*

686. The priest is holding a host in one hand and either the paten or chalice in the other. The GIRM and OM do not say what he does with the vessel while he consumes the Body of Christ. Apparently, he continues to hold it while he eats. *696*

687. The Communion chant begins as soon as the priest and people have made their responses (OM 136; GIRM 86, 159). *693, 702*

Immediate Preparation and the Body of Christ

688. The priest says another private prayer to prepare to receive the
670, 694 Body of Christ (OM 133; GIRM 158).

689. The priest is to turn toward the altar, but this rubric is unnecessary
67 if the altar is freestanding as expected (GIRM 299).

690. This is one of the private prayers of preparation to help the priest
exercise his ministry with greater devotion (GIRM 33). It is not to be
prayed aloud. The people are not supposed to answer "Amen."

691. The priest consumes the Body of Christ (OM 133; GIRM 85; 158).
He is to do so reverently. No number of external rubrics can accomplish
this alone. The priest should have a sincere reverence for Christ in his
653 heart as he receives Communion.

692. The priest is bound to receive Communion from bread consecrated
at the same Mass (GIRM 85). The Mass is a sacrifice of elements brought to
the altar, consecrated and shared. The unfolding of this sacrifice demands
that at least the priest, and preferably all the people, receive Communion
516 from the bread and wine consecrated at the Mass they attend.

693. The Communion chant begins as the priest receives Communion
(OM 136; GIRM 86, 159). The singing is meant to unite the Communion
687, 702 of all the faithful.

Immediate Preparation and the Blood of Christ

694. The priest says yet another private prayer to prepare to receive the
670, 688 Blood of Christ (OM 133; GIRM 158).

695. This is another of the private prayers of preparation to help the
priest exercise his ministry with greater devotion (GIRM 33). It is not to
be prayed aloud. The people are not supposed to answer "Amen." The
693 singing at Communion will cover this private prayer.

696. The priest consumes the Blood of Christ reverently (OM 133; GIRM
691 85; 158).

697. The use of the pall is optional (GIRM 142, 118c), but if the priest
109, 656 re-covered the chalice with it after the commingling, he needs to remove
it for Communion. The OM and GIRM make no reference to the pall at
this time.

698. In practice, when the priest receives Communion from the chalice, he swallows the particle he dropped into it at the commingling. *654* Sometimes he does not. Often he is using a chalice that others from the assembly will share, and the quantity of the consecrated wine makes it unpredictable if he will swallow the particle with his sip. Some priests consecrate only a small amount of wine in their own chalice and consume it all at this time together with the particle of consecrated bread, but the sign of Communion is weakened if the priest alone drinks from one cup. If necessary, other priests allow another communicant to consume the particle when he or she drinks from the chalice.

699. In practice, the priest usually wipes the rim of the chalice with the purificator after he drinks. The documents are silent about this, but it *110, 737* is commonly practiced and especially sanitary if others will be sharing from the same cup. Some priests dab their lips with the same purificator, but this should not be necessary. Customarily, no one else drinking from the chalice does this.

700. If the priest is wearing a wireless microphone, he switches it off as soon as his hands are free.

Communion Chant

701. The Communion chant is the song that accompanies the sharing of Communion. "Its purpose is to express the communicants' union in spirit by means of the unity of their voices, to show joy of heart, and to highlight more clearly the 'communitarian' nature of the procession to receive Communion" (GIRM 86).

702. The music begins with the priest's Communion (OM 136; GIRM 86, 159). The musicians are to start it right after the people have said, "Lord I am not worthy." This unifies the Communion of all participants *687, 693,* and allows the song to gain some footing before members of the faith- *723* ful begin to move. This works smoothly if musicians share Communion last. In some parishes musicians come to Communion first after the altar ministers, and they do not begin the music until they return to their places. This assures from the beginning that their Communion will not be overlooked and allows music to continue seamlessly from the end of Communion to the period of thanksgiving. However, it fails to unite *778* musically the Communion of the priest and the people. At Masses with several musicians, they may take turns going to Communion so that at least one of them can lead the music throughout.

703. In the United States there are several options for the Communion song (GIRM 87). The Missal supplies the text of an antiphon for every Mass. The *Graduale Romanum* supplies chant notation for singing that text in Latin. It also cites psalm verses to be sung in alternation with the repeated antiphon. This option gets little use. But the same texts may be used "in another musical setting," and vernacular settings of these texts are often available in published materials, though they are not often linked to specific Sundays. The *Graduale Simplex* offers a selection of antiphons and psalms for the seasons of the year and for specific days. An English translation is available in Paul F. Ford's *By Flowing Waters*. The Communion chant more frequently is "a song from another collection of psalms and antiphons," approved by the conference of bishops or the local bishop. Such music may be in antiphonal or metrical forms. Antiphonal forms usually work better because people are moving in procession, and many of them will be using their hands to receive Communion; it is simpler for them not to carry a book with a lengthy metrical text, but to sing from memory a shorter refrain. Finally, another "suitable liturgical song" may be sung by the choir alone or by the choir or cantor with the people. Songs of adoration are not appropriate, because they disengage singers from the communitarian nature of the procession (cf. GIRM 86). "Any psalm or other hymn is appropriate if it expresses the spiritual unity of the communicants, shows the joy of all, and makes the Communion procession an act of union of brothers and sisters in Christ" (IOM 137).

136–139,
410

704. In practice, the assembly often sings the Communion hymn poorly. People are understandably focused on receiving Communion. The procession involves everyone, and its mechanics often take people's attention away from the music. This frustrates the purpose of the chant, which is to express unity at the time of heightened communion. Singing usually works better in parishes where people remain standing after the *Lamb of God*. If each person kneels before Communion, stands for the procession, and returns to his or her place to kneel, it is hard to get a sense that Communion is an act of the community. But where people stand, the singing is usually enhanced.

669

705. If Communion lasts an unusually long time, more than one song may be sung. Ordinarily, songs of sufficient length to match the Communion procession are ideal. "Although several Communion songs may be sung in succession, depending on the length of Communion, it may be preferable to interrupt congregational singing with periods of silence, instrumental music (in seasons when it is not excluded), or choral music,

resuming the singing after an interlude" (IOM 137). Instruments are not to play solos during Lent, except on the Fourth Sunday, solemnities, and feasts (GIRM 313).

706. The music lasts throughout the distribution of Communion, but it may end sooner if a song of thanksgiving is to follow (GIRM 86). In many parishes the music continues until the leftover Communion breads have been reposed in the tabernacle, but there is no such cue in the OM or GIRM. The singing is meant to accompany the sharing of Communion. If the musicians receive Communion last, the Communion song naturally ends as the procession ends.

751, 763

702

707. The Communion antiphon may be recited (GIRM 87). All the faithful or a group of them may recite it together. If they do not, the lector reads it (198), though not from the ambo (309). Sometimes the priest recites the antiphon alone; if he does so, he leads it after he receives Communion and before distributing to the faithful (87). It seems awkward to break up Communion this way. The text may also be used "as a focus for the period of silence after Communion" (IOM 65). But singing is always preferable (GIRM 40).

73

141

DEACON'S COMMUNION

708. If there is a deacon, the priest gives him Communion under both forms (GIRM 182). The priest receives first; the deacon, second. The deacon does not receive with the priest, as a concelebrant would. In the pre-2002 GIRM (137), if Communion was distributed under both forms, the deacon received only the Body of Christ at this time, ministered the cup to the people, and then drank from the cup last. Now he is to receive both forms at the same time.

EXTRAORDINARY MINISTERS OF HOLY COMMUNION

709. When additional priests and deacons are not present and when the number of communicants warrants establishing additional stations for administering the sacrament, extraordinary ministers of Holy Communion may assist (GIRM 162, 284a). Instituted acolytes are included in this category, but most parishes use other members of the lay faithful appointed for this task.

94

710. The IOM explains that Communion ministers help "if a particularly large number are to receive Holy Communion . . . so that the rite is not

unduly long" (19). In practice, though, the ministers serve an additional purpose. They show the diversity and cohesion of the different orders, offices, and participation of the people of God (GIRM 91).

711. The IOM notes, "A sufficient number of ministers should assist in the distribution of Holy Communion" (136). But the NDR cautions that "their number should not be increased beyond what is required for the orderly and reverent distribution of the Body and Blood of the Lord" (28), and they are used "if . . . required by pastoral need" (38). RS issues a similar concern: "Only when there is a necessity may extraordinary ministers assist the Priest celebrant in accordance with the norm of law" (88), and "a brief prolongation [of the Mass] . . . is not at all a sufficient reason" (158). The OM never mentions extraordinary ministers. The Roman norms make it appear that the need for Communion ministers is unusual, but in fact the need is nearly universal in parish Sunday Masses, and the benefits are many.

712. When the need is there but Communion ministers are absent, the priest may depute a minister of Communion for a single occasion from among the faithful present (GIRM 162; IOM 20). The prayer for this circumstance is in the Missal's third appendix.

713. Ministers approach the altar after the priest has received Communion (GIRM 162; NDR 38). In some parishes the ministers enter the sanctuary at the sign of peace and stand apart from the altar until this
644   time. In some parishes the Communion ministers wash their hands on their way to the altar. Some find this extra step of hygiene a matter of courtesy, but others deem it unnecessary. The rubrics do not call for the ministers to wash their hands.

714. Lay ministers are not to receive Communion "in the manner of a concelebrating priest" (NDR 39). The IOM explains that this means they are not to self-communicate (136). It may also mean that they are
855   to receive Communion after the priest, not together with him.

715. The ministers receive Communion from the priest or deacon (NDR 38) and consume the Body and Blood of Christ. The GIRM, so careful in its descriptions of the Communion of the priest, the deacon, and the faithful, so cautious in limiting the duties of Communion ministers, never explains how or when the extraordinary ministers receive Communion.

716. A priest or deacon hands a vessel to each Communion minister (GIRM 162; NDR 39). If there are many ministers, a few of them, having

received Communion and their vessels from the priest or deacon, could help distribute Communion to the others. A priest or deacon then hands these others their vessels.

717.   Ministers of the chalice will each need a purificator (286). The GIRM never says how they get one. Customarily, the priest or deacon hands a purificator with each chalice. If he opens the purificator first, it will encourage the minister to use the entire cloth, not just a small part of it. Ministers could pick up a purificator themselves, but they usually receive one.

718.   The priest and ministers go to their Communion stations. If the Missal has not yet been removed from the altar, this would be an appropriate time for a server to do so. In theory, it may be left on the altar *651* if the priest is going to purify vessels there and if he needs the text for his private prayer. Otherwise, the Missal serves no purpose and distracts *773* from the relationship between the altar and the Communion of the faithful. If a bookstand was used for the Missal, it could be removed at this time as well. The corporal could also be removed if the vessels are not to be purified at the altar after Communion. A minister could fold it in on itself to collect any fragments and carry it from the altar to the credence table or sacristy. *70, 107, 774*

COMMUNION OF THE FAITHFUL

719.   The faithful prepare for their Communion in silent prayer (GIRM 84) and in common song (86).

Both Kinds

720.   Communion under both kinds is encouraged. "Holy Communion has a fuller form as a sign when it is distributed under both kinds. For in this form the sign of the Eucharistic banquet is more clearly evident and clear expression is given to the divine will by which the new and eternal Covenant is ratified in the Blood of the Lord, as also the relationship between the Eucharistic banquet and the eschatological banquet in the Father's kingdom" (GIRM 281). "This clearer form of the sacramental sign offers a particular opportunity of deepening the understanding of the mystery in which the faithful take part" (14). "It is most desirable that the faithful . . . partake of the chalice (cf. no. 283), so that even by means of the signs Communion will stand out more clearly as a participation in the sacrifice actually being celebrated" (85). "The faithful should be

encouraged to seek to participate more eagerly in this sacred rite, by which
442, 851 the sign of the Eucharistic banquet is made more fully evident" (282).

Procession

721. The priest takes the paten or ciborium and goes from the altar to the people for Communion (OM 134; GIRM 160). The deacon administers the chalice (GIRM 182). In practice, other ministers carry their vessels to their stations, and the faithful approach in procession.

722. In the United States the faithful are to stand for Communion (GIRM 160). If they have remained standing after the *Lamb of God,* they simply
669 retain their posture throughout the Communion rite. Before the Council it was traditional for those receiving Communion to kneel at a rail separating the nave from the sanctuary. Today a rail no longer serves a purpose. Still, if anyone wishes to kneel for Communion, he or she may do so. But the sense of Communion will be better expressed if all retain "a common posture," demonstrating their oneness as they process toward the banquet of life (42).

723. Musicians will need to receive Communion. "Care should be taken that singers, too, can receive Communion with ease" (GIRM 86). Actually, instrumentalists deserve the same care. They may come last, first, or staggered throughout the Communion procession. Ideally, the Communion chant begins with the priest's Communion (OM 136; GIRM 86,
702 159), suggesting that musicians best receive last.

724. In the United States ushers may assist with processions (IOM 23). In some parishes, they stand in the center aisle and guide people toward the front, row by row. But regular participants do not need this much direction, and the ushers may be more a distraction than a help.

725. Ideally, Communion stations should be arranged close to the altar. In some churches, stations are established in the balcony, by the entry, or even in the middle of a long aisle. Some people incongruously process away from the altar and toward the door to receive Communion. People are being fed from a common table, and the procession should move toward it, close to it.

The Body of Christ

726. In the United States each person, before receiving Communion, is to bow the head "as a gesture of reverence" (GIRM 160). Even right after

the Council, each communicant was asked to make some gesture of reverence before receiving Communion, but this rubric was largely ignored. Many people thought that approaching the altar in slow procession and coming to Communion with open hands or open mouths, like beggars, already demonstrated reverence for the sacrament. Some of the faithful did nothing more; others, upon reaching the Communion station, bowed the head, made a profound bow, or even genuflected. Many others made a sign of the cross *after* receiving Communion. To standardize the practice, the American bishops called for a bow of the head in the 2002 GIRM. The practice still varies. Some communicants make a profound bow. They see the priest and ministers make a profound bow to the altar, so they presume that the gesture of reverence to the Body and Blood of Christ should be at least the same. However, the rubric is much simpler. It is only a bow of the head, the same bow made when pronouncing the name of Jesus (275a).

727. The rubric does not explicitly state when the sign of reverence is to be given. Some make it while the person ahead is receiving Communion. Others do so upon arriving at the station. Still others give it while answering "Amen." To assign each element of the ritual its time, the sign of reverence probably belongs when the communicant has reached the station and before the priest or minister says, "The Body of Christ." But the governing principle is to come to Communion reverently, and that allows some variation in external practice.

728. As each person arrives at the station and has made the gesture of reverence, the priest holds a piece of the consecrated bread up a bit over the vessel, shows it to the communicant and says, "The Body of Christ" (OM 134; GIRM 161). A deacon who distributes the Body of Christ does so the same way a priest does (OM 134; GIRM 171e, 182), and the same is true of extraordinary ministers. Some ministers have varied the formula, but the specified words are most powerful in this unadorned acclamation. Some ministers call the communicant by name, but this needless personalization can easily offend those whose name is unknown or misstated, and it breaks the mantra-like proclamation. The ritual formula is the most profound, especially when it is repeated exactly the same way, time and time again, Mass after Mass, church by church. Many ministers establish eye contact with the communicant to deepen the sincerity of this brief dialogue. 302

729. The communicant responds, "Amen" (OM 134; GIRM 161). Ideally, this response should be made strongly and confidently. In practice, some communicants mumble it. Others omit it, or substitute a text such as

"Thank you"—well-meaning, but inappropriate. No other conversation is appropriate.

730. In the United States the minister places the consecrated bread either in the hand or on the tongue of the communicant. Communicants generally indicate this by presenting their open hands visibly or by lifting their head, opening their mouth, and extending their tongue. When receiving the Body of Christ in the hand, communicants are not to reach out and take it from the ministers with their fingers (GIRM 160); they are

743 to receive it in the palm. Placing one hand beneath the other is probably the best way. The person receiving Communion in the hand should step aside and pause to consume it, making way for the next person and not eating on the run. Whether receiving in the hand or on the tongue, the communicant consumes the consecrated bread entirely (161).

731. "The Communion-plate for the Communion of the faithful should be retained, so as to avoid the danger of the sacred host or some fragment of it falling" (RS 93). Traditionally, a server held the communion-plate beneath the chin of those kneeling at the rail to receive Communion in the mouth. The GIRM's only references to the communion-plate place it on the credence table before Mass (118c) and in the hands of those receiving Communion by intinction, never in the hands of a server (287). RS footnotes GIRM 118c, the placement of the communion-plate on the credence table, to argue that its use should be retained. But with so many people receiving Communion in the hand and the customary care given to Communion, it

114, 741 could easily get in the way. At papal Masses the master of ceremonies has held the communion-plate for those receiving Communion in the mouth, but not for those receiving Communion in the hand from the pope. Priests, hundreds of whom sometimes distribute the Body of Christ at a papal Mass, have not been accompanied by servers with communion-plates.

732. Sometimes a minister uses up his or her supply of consecrated bread while people are still in line. Traditionally the minister breaks a few hosts before they are gone to make sure that everyone can receive from bread consecrated at that Mass. Sometimes the minister routes people to another Communion station. If necessary, the minister retrieves previously consecrated breads from the tabernacle, but ideally this does not

666 take place during the Communion procession.

733. The GIRM presumes that a deacon who assists with Communion will administer the chalice to the faithful (182). The OM acknowledges that the deacon assists in offering Communion (134) and that Communion may be given under both kinds, but it refers the reader elsewhere for the procedure (135). The details are in GIRM 161 and 284–287. If there is no deacon, an instituted acolyte offers the chalice to the faithful (191). In practice, this ministry is commonly assigned to deacons and extraordinary lay ministers of Communion.

734. After receiving the Body of Christ, the communicant moves to the next station and stands facing the minister of the chalice (GIRM 286). He or she bows the head as a gesture of reverence (160). The minister holds out the cup, shows it to the communicant and says, "The Blood of Christ" (286). The communicant responds, "Amen" (286).

302, 728, 729

735. The communicant takes the chalice into his or her own hands. For reasons of health, a person who cannot tolerate gluten must not receive from the presider's cup, into which a particle of the consecrated bread was dropped. "The minister hands over the chalice, which the communicant raises to his or her mouth" (GIRM 286). Both people exercise the greatest care that the vessel is handed over comfortably and securely. In some other ecclesial communities, the minister holds the cup and tips it into the communicant's mouth. This is not the practice in the Catholic Church, where it seems more normal for the communicant to hold the cup while drinking and where the danger of spilling the Blood of Christ is thus minimized.

430, 443

736. "Each communicant drinks a little from the chalice" (GIRM 286). This probably means a sip, not a gulp, not a wetting of the lips. It should reverently resemble drinking.

737. The communicant hands the cup back to the minister and goes to his or her place (GIRM 286). The minister wipes the rim of the chalice with a purificator. In practice, the minister usually also rotates the cup for the next communicant and uses a fresh part of the purificator for each wipe.

110, 699

738. Communicants do not give Communion to each other (GIRM 160). This is particularly an issue with the chalice, a vessel that any communicant may hold. Everyone receives Communion from a minister, not from another communicant.

739. If the cup is emptied before all have received, the minister has several options. At some parishes additional consecrated wine remains on the altar, and the minister replaces the empty cup with a full one. Otherwise the minister routes communicants to another line or sends them back to their places without having received. The quantity of wine prepared for a future Mass may need to be adjusted.

446

740. For reasons of ill health a communicant may abstain from the chalice.

Intinction, Tube, Spoon

741. Communion under both forms may also be administered by intinction (GIRM 287). The communicant holds the communion-plate under his or her chin and bows the head as a gesture of reverence. A minister holding a chalice stands near the priest, who holds a vessel of consecrated bread. Combination cup-plate vessels are manufactured, but these liturgical documents do not refer to them. The priest dips a host partly into the chalice, shows it to the communicant, and says, "The Body and Blood of Christ." The communicant responds, "Amen," receives the sacrament in the mouth, and returns to his or her place. Logically, the communicant would pass the communion-plate to the next communicant before leaving the area.

114, 726,
731

434

742. The GIRM mentions only a priest as the minister of Communion by intinction (287). This may be an oversight, or it may imply there is no need for another minister when the priest gives Communion under both kinds. The IOM, however, refers more generically to "the minister" who gives Communion by intinction (136).

743. A communicant is not to receive the host in the hand and personally dip it into the chalice (RS 104). This custom is observed in other ecclesial communities, but it has never been part of Catholic Communion practice. Some communicants persist in this, even though it has never been approved. It would be charitable to correct such a communicant after Mass, not during Communion. Self-intinction heightens concerns about sanitation during the Communion rite. Further, the Catholic Church maintains a distinction between the minister and the communicant. The communicant always receives and never takes Communion. It comes as gift.

730

744. A communicant receives by intinction only in the mouth and never receives the intincted host in the hand (RS 104). This helps prevent dripping the Blood of Christ.

745. The Blood of Christ may also be administered by means of a tube or a spoon (GIRM 245), but this practice is not customary in the Roman Rite in the United States.

Blessings

746. In some parishes children too young for First Communion and adults who are unable to receive Communion present themselves in the Communion line for a blessing from the minister. Some priests invite them. The practice has no provision in any liturgical document, universal or national. Proponents hold that it makes everyone feel included in Communion, but there is a big difference between sharing Communion and receiving a blessing. The blessing at the end of Mass need not be anticipated during the Communion rite.

807

Returning to Seats

747. After receiving Communion, the faithful return to their seats. The GIRM's only reference to this obvious practice is in the description of Communion under both forms. After the communicant receives from the chalice, he or she returns to his or her place (287). There is no such instruction after receiving under one form (161).

748. This seemingly innocuous omission sets up a more practical question: What posture do the faithful take upon returning to their places? The universal GIRM asked everyone to stand from after the consecration until the end of Mass, unless they sit for the period of thanksgiving after Communion (43). In the United States the GIRM permits the faithful to kneel after the *Lamb of God* but asks them to stand for Communion. In practice, many of the faithful return to their places and kneel or sit, although these postures have never been called for. The CDWDS attempted to clarify the matter in a later statement permitting these devotional postures after each person receives Communion. The intent of GIRM 43 is "on the one hand, to ensure within broad limits a certain uniformity of posture within the congregation for the various parts of the celebration of Holy Mass, and on the other, not to regulate posture rigidly in such a way that those who wish to kneel or sit would no longer be free" (Prot. N. 855/03/L). However, this did not eliminate the posture the GIRM had in mind all along, namely, standing. The documents, therefore, permit three different postures after receiving Communion.

749. The Communion rite would maintain more unanimity and expressiveness if, with the bishop's permission, the faithful remained standing after the *Lamb of God* until everyone had received Communion. Each would wait his or her turn standing, process standing, receive Communion standing, and return to his or her place standing, all the while singing the Communion chant and expressing solidarity with those who are yet to receive.

669

750. In practice, some communicants never return to their seats. They leave the church after receiving Communion. Some come to Communion carrying car keys, purses, or jackets. Liturgical documents do not envision a self-dismissal of the faithful during the Communion rite, which breaks the unity of the Body of Christ at its most focused moment. The widespread practice indicates that many of the faithful poorly appreciate the meaning of Communion and the value of the closing rites of the Mass. Many parish priests find it dispiriting that RS never lists this among liturgical abuses.

827

751. Once all have received, the Communion song comes to an end (GIRM 86). Many people assume that Communion ends when the tabernacle door is shut or when the priest sits down, but Communion ends when the last person has received.

706, 763

After Communion

Communion to the Sick and Homebound

752. Communion ministers may prepare vessels to bring Communion to the sick. "In accord with an ancient tradition, it is appropriate for Holy Communion to be taken directly from the Sunday Mass to the sick and to those unable to leave their homes" (IOM 21).

753. The practice varies considerably among churches. The IOM says, "The priest gives the pyx containing the Holy Eucharist to the deacons, acolytes, or extraordinary ministers of Holy Communion immediately after Communion has been distributed" (IOM 21). But it is not so simple. Some parishes bring Communion to dozens, even hundreds of people each weekend. The priest would need to have empty pyxes brought to the altar either during the breaking of the bread or at the conclusion of Communion. He would need to know how many Communion breads to place in each pyx, and which ones go to which ministers. The Church also permits bringing Communion under the form of wine to those who cannot swallow food (PCS 74). The GIRM and IOM do not refer to this practice.

650

754. There are other options. In some parishes the Communion ministers retrieve the Communion breads they need from the tabernacle after the Mass. But this breaks the connection between the Mass and the Communion of the homebound. In other parishes those bringing Communion to the sick bring a pyx with them when they come to receive Communion, whether in the sanctuary or the procession of the faithful. They hold the pyx open to the minister and indicate the number of hosts they need. The minister places that many in the pyx. The one bringing Communion to the sick closes the lid, places the pyx in a pocket, and then receives Communion from the minister.

755. If Communion is to be brought to the sick under the form of wine, the vessel should probably be brought to the altar and filled at the preparation of the gifts. The wine is consecrated together with that in chalices. The priest hands it to a Communion minister after Communion. If this vessel resembles a flask or jar, the minister may screw on the lid in the sacristy.   *445, 469*

756. The IOM allows Communion ministers to the sick and homebound to leave after receiving Communion themselves or as part of the concluding procession of ministers (21). Neither suggestion has any special   *161, 824* merit. There is no dismissal during the Communion rite, even though many of the faithful excuse themselves. The concluding procession is   *750* much simpler than the one that begins the Mass, and including at the end Communion ministers who were excluded at the beginning seems inappropriate (21). The Communion ministers who bring Communion to homes are not necessarily the same group who distributed Communion to the faithful at the Mass. More meaningfully, Communion ministers to the sick and homebound leave with the rest of the assembly, all of whom will be sent to serve the mission of the Church in the world.

Consuming the Remains

757. The priest and deacon may consume what remains of Communion at the altar (GIRM 163, 182, 279). They may consume both the Body and Blood of Christ. Although it is customary to place leftover Communion breads in the tabernacle, they may be consumed at the altar.   *446*

758. Extraordinary ministers of Communion "may consume what remains of the Precious Blood from their chalice of distribution with permission of the diocesan bishop" (NDR 52). The IOM overlooks the local bishop's permission with a blanket statement: "When extraordinary ministers of Holy Communion are present, they may consume what remains of the Precious

Blood from their chalice of distribution" (21). This prudent permission allows several ministers to reverently consume what remains of the Precious Blood without facing the deleterious effects of the properties of alcohol. By extension, the ministers could also help consume what remains of the consecrated bread to minimize the amount stored in the tabernacle.

759. The documents do not say where the Communion ministers consume what remains of the Body and Blood of Christ. In practice, many of them eat or drink at the station where they have been ministering, and this is often the simplest and most reverent solution. Others go to the sacristy. Still others return to the altar, where the GIRM envisions that the priest and deacon consume the remains.

760. It is never permitted to pour leftover consecrated wine on the ground or into the sacrarium (NDR 55; IOM 138; Code of Canon Law 1367).

771

Reposition

761. The remaining Communion breads may be placed in the tabernacle. The GIRM's only reference to this comes from its treatment of Mass without a deacon. It says of the remaining consecrated hosts that the priest "either consumes them at the altar or carries them to the place designated for the reservation of the Eucharist" (163). In theory, the hosts need not be returned to the altar; they could be brought directly to the place of reposition. But the IOM envisions that they are brought first to the altar, where the priest or deacon gathers and distributes them into ciboria (21).

762. In practice, many parishes assign the reposition of the Eucharist to Eucharistic ministers or deacons. The trend of Roman documents has been to limit the service of Communion ministers, but there is no clear reason why the priest alone should repose the Blessed Sacrament after Communion, especially if the tabernacle is located in a separate chapel for private adoration (GIRM 315).

667

763. In practice, the closing of the tabernacle door has signaled the music to stop and the faithful to be seated, but there is no such rubric. Music stops when the last communicant has received, just as it begins when the first does. If musicians receive Communion last, the music stops in time for them to join the procession. If people are to sit after Communion, they may do so after all have received. Especially in parishes where the tabernacle is in a separate chapel, the closing of the door need provide no signal for posture (GIRM 315).

702
778
128, 706,
751

148

764. At the altar the priest gathers any fragments that may remain (GIRM 163). The deacon may assist (183). This probably refers to fragments on the corporal or in various empty vessels left on it. Traditionally the fragments are gathered into a chalice. In practice, many priests leave the gathering of fragments to the ministers who perform the purification of vessels in the sacristy after Mass.

828

765. The vessels used for Communion are to be purified. The priest, a deacon, or an instituted acolyte may clean them (OM 137; GIRM 163, 171e, 183, 192, 279, 284b). The purification takes place either at the altar or at the credence table. The credence table is preferred (279). If the deacon purifies the vessels at the credence table, the priest goes to his chair (283). *777* If the purification is done at the altar, the IOM suggests "at the side of the altar rather than at the center" (138).

766. The documents seem to envision that only two vessels were used when it calls for the priest, deacon, or acolyte to purify the paten or ciborium over the chalice and the chalice itself (GIRM 163; OM 137). In practice, there may have been many more.

767. In the United States extraordinary ministers of Holy Communion received permission to assist in the purification of vessels if the bishop grants the faculty for a grave reason (CDWDS Prot. 1383/01/L, March 22, 2002). The USCCB requested an extension of the indult, which was originally approved for three years. Communion ministers had been purifying vessels for some years prior to this permission, and it surprised many of them that an indult was necessary for this service. In many parishes there are a number of vessels to be purified, and ministers are quite competent for the task. It is not clear why a "grave reason" would be necessary for a priest to share this simple ministry.

768. "The paten is usually wiped clean with the purificator" (GIRM 279). Logically, the same would apply to other vessels used to distribute the Body of Christ.

718

769. "The purification of the chalice is done with water alone or with wine and water, which is then drunk by whoever does the purification" (GIRM 279). Prior to the Second Vatican Council, the purification always included both water and wine. Wine diluted any remaining contents, so that it no longer could be identified as the Blood of Christ. Water was used for cleansing. Although some parishes retain the practice of purifying with wine first, it is unnecessary and foreign to the normal use of wine.

770. Water is needed, but the documents do not explain how it gets to the altar if the purification takes place there. Customarily, a server brings the water cruet to the minister. If purification takes place at the credence table, the water is already there.

771. Not all the water need be consumed, especially if the purification takes place in the sacristy. Customarily, the first rinse of the chalice is swallowed. Then hot water and soap are used to wash the vessels. Subsequent rinses are poured into the sacrarium (GIRM 334), and the vessels are dried. A sacrarium is a special sink in the sacristy with a pipe leading directly into the earth. Some municipalities may not permit them. The sacrarium was not required after the Second Vatican Council, but its use was restored in the 2002 GIRM. It is never permitted to pour leftover consecrated wine on the ground or into the sacrarium (NDR 55; IOM *760* 138; Code of Canon Law 1367).

772. Customarily the cups are dried with a purificator, though the documents never indicate this.

773. While a priest purifies the vessels, he offers a prayer that even these fragments will purify the mind and provide the benefits of eternity (OM 138; GIRM 163). Other ministers are not expected to recite this text when they purify vessels. It is among those private prayers calling the priest to exercise his ministry with greater devotion (GIRM 33). Still, any minister who purifies vessels should do so respectfully and prayerfully.

774. If the vessels were purified at the altar, a server carries them to the credence table (GIRM 163). If the corporal is still on the altar, this would be an appropriate time to fold and move it off the altar to the credence *70, 107* table. If the Missal is still on the altar, it may be removed, along with the *651, 718,* bookstand if one was used.
784

775. After the vessels are purified, they are arranged (GIRM 171e, 183, 192, 284b). The GIRM does not further explain this, but it probably means they are arranged into the traditional stack of vessels—chalice on the bottom, then purificator, paten, pall, and chalice veil—which looks neat *112* but bears no resemblance to the arrangement of parallel items in real life. If multiple vessels were used, no special arrangement seems necessary. But vessels should not be stacked irreverently.

764, 828 776. The purification of vessels may take place in the sacristy after Mass. If this option is followed, they are "suitably covered on a corporal, either *107, 131* at the altar or at the credence table" (GIRM 163, 183). Palls and purificators supply suitable cover. It will be less distracting if the vessels are set on the credence table instead of the altar. The contents should have been consumed or put away in the tabernacle before the vessels are covered.

THANKSGIVING

777. The priest may go to his chair (OM 138; GIRM 164). He is already there if someone else has purified the vessels. The rubrics permit him *765* to finish the Mass at the altar, but going to the chair helps the priest to resume his presidential role for the conclusion of the service and better suits the functions of chair and altar.

64, 75, 784

778. The entire assembly may observe a period of silence for private prayer (OM 138; GIRM 43, 45, 88, 164). They may sit or kneel during this time. In practice, many of the Catholic faithful kneel for a while as soon as they return to their places after Communion, and then sit. But this disrupts the common posture, action, and song of the Communion rite. The rubrics envisioned the community standing throughout the distribution of Communion and then sitting or kneeling together after Communion. In many parishes, though, people who are still kneeling *706, 748,* sit when the priest sits or when the tabernacle door is closed. *749, 763*

779. Alternatively, a psalm, canticle, or another hymn may be sung (OM 138; GIRM 88, 164). GIRM 88 says that it is sung "by the entire congregation," but the other citations omit that qualifier. Sometimes a choir sings an anthem here. Although some parishes call it a "meditation song," its purpose is really thanksgiving. If a concluding song is to be inserted into the liturgy, a thanksgiving song at this time may seem superfluous. In *820* practice, most parishes choose a period of silence over a hymn. Having just sung at Communion, people seem to prefer a little silence. Some parishes sing a hymn after Communion instead of the Communion chant. Singing during Communion is difficult for many communities, but it is preferred. The references to sitting or kneeling after Communion are for *701* the period of silence (GIRM 43, 45). If the people are to sing instead, they will do so more attentively and excellently if they stand.

780. There is another option: no silence or hymn at all. The priest may proceed immediately to the prayer after Communion. But the sacrament of Communion deserves a word of thanks to God.

781. Some parishes interrupt the silence after Communion with other activities. Some take up the second collection at this time. Some make *416*

announcements. Others conduct devotions. None of these actions is appropriate to the purpose of the liturgy at this point. This is a time for silence and praise.

PRAYER AFTER COMMUNION

782. The priest leads the people in a prayer after Communion (OM 139; GIRM 165). This brings "to completion the prayer of the People of God" and concludes the entire Communion rite (GIRM 89).

783. All stand (GIRM 43). In practice, people often wait until the priest says, "Let us pray," as if he is saying, "Let us stand." If the people stand as soon as the priest does, they more readily enter into a spirit of prayer at his invitation. If the server brings the Missal forward when the priest stands,
786 it will eliminate a distraction when people should be focusing on prayer.

75 784. The priest stands "at the chair or at the altar" (GIRM 165). After the Vatican Council the OM said the same. The 2002 OM reverses the order of these options, allowing him to stand at the altar or at the chair (139). The OM, which frequently envisions the priest saying Mass with his back to the people, prefers him to remain at the altar for the end of Mass. Even the IOM notes that the chair is an optional site for the hom-
361 ily and the prayer after Communion (54). However, in a typical Sunday assembly, where the altar and chair are differentiated, where the chair is the presidential seat, the chair is the more appropriate place for the
765, 777 priest to stand after Communion.

785. Both OM 139 and GIRM 165 indicate that the priest should now be "facing the people." This expression presumes a situation where the priest has been saying Mass with his back to the people and where he is concluding Mass at an altar fixed against the back wall, even though the GIRM calls for a freestanding altar (GIRM 299). If the priest is at the chair, this rubric is unnecessary. The chair is supposed to be in a place
67, 76 facing the people (310).

783 786. The priest says, "Let us pray" (OM 139; GIRM 165). The priest is
255 to have his hands joined, as for the invitation to pray the collect. Some priests find it more natural to briefly open their hands, as they do when
503 addressing the people for the invitation before the prayer over the gifts
631 and at the greeting of peace.

787. A brief period of silence follows this invitation to prayer only if there was no silence preceding it (OM 139; GIRM 165). Communion may

have been followed by a hymn or by no silence at all. In those cases a brief period of silence follows "Let us pray." *779, 780*

788. For the prayer, the priest extends his hands (OM 139; GIRM 165). This is the same gesture he used at the collect and for other presidential prayers. He prays the text from the Missal for the Mass of the day. *263, 509, 620*

789. GIRM 89 points out that the priest says only one Communion prayer. Prior to the Council there were occasions when he said more than one. This reminder should no longer be necessary. *262, 510*

790. At Masses with children the priest is free to choose another prayer more suited to children, keeping in mind the season of the year (DMC 50). He may even adapt the texts to help the children understand their meaning (DMC 51).

791. If the end of the prayer includes the name of Jesus, the priest is to bow his head (GIRM 275a), though many priests do not.

792. Singing this prayer is encouraged (GIRM 40). In practice it is rarely *141* sung, but the first appendix of the Missal suggests a tone for chanting the prayer after Communion.

793. All acclaim "Amen" to the short conclusion of the prayer after Communion (OM 139; GIRM 89, 165), making its words their own. *267*

Closing Rites

ANNOUNCEMENTS

781, 811

794. Brief announcements may be made if necessary (OM 140; GIRM 90a, 166, 184). These should follow the prayer after Communion. Some parishes make the announcements while everyone sits after Communion. This disturbs the period of silence and invites longer announcements. The prayer after Communion concludes the Communion rites. The announcements introduce the closing rites.

364

795. Announcements should not be made at another time before or during the Mass. "Any necessary announcements are to be kept completely separate from the homily; they must take place following the prayer after Communion" (LM 27).

360

796. The documents never mention these announcements without saying that they should be "brief" and made only if necessary (OM 140; GIRM 90a, 166, 184). In practice, most parishes find announcements are indeed necessary to highlight upcoming events. But they sometimes fail in brevity. The content is best limited to events of interest in the coming week. They need not detail times, places, and contact information. Sometimes, though, a longer announcement may be important, such as a report from a committee or an appeal for extra help. "If the need arises for the gathered faithful to be given instruction or testimony by a layperson in a Church concerning the Christian life . . . for serious reasons it is permissible that this type of instruction or testimony be given after the Priest has proclaimed the Prayer after Communion" (RS 74).

797. The GIRM recommends that announcements be made by the deacon unless the priest prefers to make them (184). Other references (OM 140; GIRM 90a, 166) do not specify who makes the announcements. The IOM says another member of the community may do so. In practice, the cantor or commentator frequently reads announcements at parishes. If the deacon is especially involved in the various ministries of the parish,

his service enriches his leadership of the prayer of the faithful and the announcements. *389*

798. People remain standing through the brief announcements (GIRM 43; IOM 143). If a longer instruction or testimony is to be given, it would be courteous to let the assembly be seated.

799. The IOM asks that the announcements not be given from the ambo (143). If the priest or deacon gives them, he need not move from his chair. A cantor or commentator could use his or her own microphone and stand. *73*

BLESSING

800. If "parish helpers" have been caring for infants elsewhere through-out the Mass, they may bring the children back to the assembly for the blessing (DMC 16). This envisions a situation where parents or guardians *49* have entrusted their infants to the care of others in a separate room.

801. The priest faces the people for the greeting (OM 141). Once again, the OM presumes that the priest has been saying Mass with his back to the people, contrary to GIRM 299. *67*

802. The priest greets the people with the words "The Lord be with you" (OM 141; GIRM 90b, 167). The priest extends his hands as he did for other greetings. The people make their response. *202, 345, 503, 539, 631*

803. If there is a deacon and if the blessing is expanded with a prayer over the people or another more solemn form of blessing, the deacon *804* commands the people to bow their heads (GIRM 185). The GIRM never says that the people actually do so (275a), but that is the intent. They should probably remain bowing throughout the blessing. It is not a bow of the body but a bow of the head.

804. The blessing may be preceded by a prayer over the people or a solemn blessing (OM 142; GIRM 90b, 167). A prayer over the people is an oration concluding with a formula that prompts the people to respond "Amen." Solemn blessings are formulas in three parts, each calling for the people to respond with an "Amen." In practice, few people do because it is difficult to pick up the cue unless the blessing is sung. Some priests use eye contact or a nod of the head to elicit the response, but with heads bowed, the people will not be looking at him. Other priests inflect their voices to prompt a reply. Or the deacon or priest may introduce the blessing with a command such as, "Bow your heads and pray for God's blessing with your Amen."

805. If the priest offers a prayer over the people or a solemn blessing, he first locates the place in the Missal. It should have been marked with a ribbon before Mass. Then he extends his hands over the people while he prays. The rubric for extending hands is found in the collection of blessings in the Missal, but it is missing from the OM and the GIRM.

806. For the Trinitarian blessing, the priest briefly joins his hands, places his left hand over his breast, and raises his right hand (GIRM 167). These rubrics are new to the 2002 GIRM. They did not even appear in the pre-Vatican II Missal. Logically, a left-handed presider would reverse hands.

807. As the priest says the words of blessing, he makes the sign of the cross over the people with his right hand (OM 141; GIRM 167). In practice, most people sign themselves with the cross at the same time (IOM 146), even though the OM and the GIRM never mention them doing it.

808. At the conclusion of the blessing, the people answer "Amen" (OM 141; GIRM 167).

809. Singing is encouraged for dialogues during the Mass (GIRM 40). The first appendix of the Missal offers a selection of sample chants for the solemn blessing and the prayer over the people. The OM provides notes on the page for the priest and people to sing the final blessing and amen (141).

DISMISSAL

810. The priest may give concluding comments before the dismissal (GIRM 31). These are part of a series of explanations he may give throughout the Mass. If he has some point he wishes to drive home, he may do so here. Few priests add more words at this time.

811. In Masses with children these comments are "important" (DMC 54). "Before they are dismissed they need some repetition and application of what they have heard." The DMC says these remarks precede the final blessing, not the dismissal, but this seems to be a mistake because it footnotes the paragraph of the GIRM treating the priest's comments before the dismissal. These comments are different from the parochial announcements before the blessing. DMC 54 does not explicitly state that the priest makes these remarks. It might be fitting for a skilled catechist to do so.

812. The deacon dismisses the assembly. In his absence the priest does (OM 144; GIRM 90c, 168, 185). The dismissal is given "so that each may

go out to do good works, praising and blessing God" (90c). The post-Vatican II Sacramentary in English imported this explanation into the OM, but in Latin the OM has never carried it.

813.   The OM, presuming again that Mass is being said with the ministers' backs to the people, notes that the deacon or priest faces the people for the dismissal (144). GIRM 185 says the same about the deacon. But both these ministers will already be facing the people if they are at their chairs and if their chairs are properly situated (310), or if they are at the altar and the altar is freestanding (299).

76, 187, 67

814.   The deacon or priest joins his hands for the dismissal (OM 144; GIRM 168, 185). This is the same gesture used for the greeting before the gospel and the invitation to offer peace.

345, 635

815.   The deacon or priest dismisses the people with the prescribed formula. The post-Vatican II Sacramentary in English gave three options for the dismissal. In practice, many clergy have dismissed the people "in these or similar words," although that option was never explicitly stated. The USCCB requested the inclusion of two alternative dismissal texts in the English translation of the third edition of the Missal.

816.   The people respond, "Thanks be to God" (OM 144; GIRM 168). These are the last spoken or sung words in the OM.

817.   Throughout the octave of Easter and on Pentecost Sunday two Alleluias are appended both to the dismissal and to its response. This is noted not in the OM or GIRM but at the end of the rubrics for the Easter Vigil and Pentecost Sunday.

818.   The singing of dialogues is encouraged (GIRM 40). The OM supplies notes on the page for the priest or deacon, and there is another sung dismissal in the first appendix of the Missal.

141

819.   The dismissal rite is omitted if some other liturgical act follows (OM 146; GIRM 170). The greeting, blessing, and dismissal are all omitted on days such as Holy Thursday and on occasions such as funerals or Eucharistic exposition. Announcements, if necessary, could still be given.

794

RECESSION

820.   No recessional hymn is noted in the OM or the GIRM. In practice, almost every parish sings one on Sundays. The IOM permits the practice

with some reluctance: "A recessional song is always optional, even for solemn occasions" (147). Most congregations instinctively feel that Mass should end as it began, with everyone singing. However, the omission of a recessional hymn lends more weight to the dismissal. The assembly is sent forth to do good works, and nothing delays them, not even a song. Another musical tradition is for the organ to play a postlude.

821. If there is a recessional hymn for all to sing, it would be courteous for the priest and deacon to remain at their chairs, singing, until the song is nearly over.

822. If the concluding rites have taken place at the chair, the priest and deacon move to the altar for the veneration.

823. The priest and deacon venerate the altar by kissiing it as they did at the beginning of the Mass (OM 145; GIRM 90d). A procession—or recession—forms. In most parishes the priest and deacon walk out behind the servers. Customarily, if servers carried the cross and candles at the beginning of Mass, they carry them out at the end, but the documents are not clear about this. The CB says that on reaching the sacristy, the ministers "lay aside the articles they have used in the celebration" (170). This presumes that they carried those articles with them—probably the cross and candles.

824. The GIRM notes that the acolyte leaves in procession (193), but it never calls for the lector to do so (194–198). If this is an instituted lector who vested and sat in the sanctuary throughout the service, he would leave with the other ministers. The Book of the Gospels has already been set aside. It is not retrieved for the recession. Communion ministers typically do not walk out in procession, but the IOM says they may do so if they are bringing Communion to the sick and homebound (21). There is no reference to the carrying of incense in the final procession (GIRM 276). There is nothing more to be incensed.

825. All the ministers forming the procession make a profound bow to the altar (OM 145; GIRM 90d). If the tabernacle is in the sanctuary, these ministers genuflect (GIRM 274). It is not clear if this should replace a bow to the altar. The documents imply that they make this reverence together, but it does not say where they should stand. In practice, many parishes have the ministers step outside the sanctuary to the head of the aisle and stand side by side for this reverence.

826. All the ministers walk out in the order in which they entered (GIRM 193). This paragraph notes that they walk to the sacristy, but in practice at some parishes they walk into a narthex or outdoors.

827. The rest of the assembly leaves. The OM and GIRM make no men- *750* tion of this. It would be appropriate for the people to make a reverence as they leave their places: a profound bow to the altar (GIRM 90d) or a genuflection to the tabernacle if it is in the sanctuary (274). Ushers prefer- *52* ably pass out parish bulletins to people as they exit. Many people sign *51* themselves with holy water upon leaving the church. The CB promotes this practice as people walk into the church (110) but says nothing about people walking out. The CB sees it only as a reminder of baptism in preparation for the Mass. People often visit among themselves or with *43* the ministers after Mass.

828. Vessels may be cleansed in the sacristy after the dismissal (GIRM 163, 183). The OM and GIRM say nothing of the purification of linens, but *131, 764,* RS asks that linens be washed first by hand, so that the first wash may *776* be poured down the sacrarium (120). RS lists this among the functions of the laity, not the clergy (44).

829. The documents make no further reference to the collection, but every parish knows the importance of placing it in a secure place im- mediately after Mass (GIRM 73, 140). For the sake of prudence, more than one person should handle the money. *455*

830. All the ministers and all the faithful are to depart in peace. They are sent forth "to do good works, praising and blessing God," until they gather for Eucharist again (GIRM 90c).

Liturgical Renewal

831. Sunday Mass underwent dramatic changes after the Second Vatican Council. The meaning of the Mass remained the same, but the reform of liturgical texts and actions was undertaken "to express more clearly the holy things they signify" (SC 21). People commonly describe the changes in two ways: the priest says Mass facing the people, and Mass is in English. But many more changes simplified the structure of the Mass and enhanced the participation of ministers and the faithful.

832. Since that time additional changes have come. More will follow. Almost all changes provoke controversy. Catholic spirituality has been grounded in stability. The changes of the 1960s restabilized the Mass, but they also announced that change is possible within the purview of Catholic spirituality. The unsettled nature of the liturgical renewal has delighted those Catholics who appreciate the flexibility and variety of worship that adjusts to culture, while it has disturbed others who see consistency as a sign of the Church's unity and of its participation in spiritual commerce with a changeless God.

833. With the publication of the third edition of the Council's Roman Missal, a number of liturgical matters are still being discussed. Some are specific; others are more general.

SOME SPECIFIC ISSUES

SHADOWS OF THE PREVIOUS MISSAL

834. The pre-Vatican II Missal still casts an outdated shadow on some rubrics. For example, the OM frequently calls for the priest and deacon to face the people. It implies that Mass is still being celebrated at an altar against the back wall of a church. Some historic churches have never installed a freestanding altar, but this is clearly not the preference of the GIRM. The OM is a central text for Catholic worship, and it would be

more helpful if it presumed the sanctuary arrangement promoted by the GIRM and adopted by most parishes around the world. By retaining these references, the OM tacitly sponsors arranging churches with an altar against the back wall. Some clear instructions need to be given for the few churches still observing the former practice, but these would be better relegated to a few paragraphs in the GIRM, not stitched into the very fabric of the OM.

835. Similarly, the GIRM and OM no longer need to remind priest and people about prayers and actions formerly performed three times, now done only once, or about the omission of spoken prayers during the blessing of incense. A full generation away from the Council, few people remember the former practices, so these instructions are unnecessary.

836. The GIRM and OM have minimized the number and kind of bows of the head from the former Missal. But they still call for the head to bow at the name of Jesus, Mary, the Trinity, and the saint in whose honor Mass is celebrated. Very few priests observe these bows. Multiple bows of the head will seem more absurd than reverent on days such as Holy Family Sunday and the Solemnity of All Saints. The usefulness of this holdover from the previous practice is questionable.

"Offertory" and "Preparation of the Gifts"

837. The word "offertory" now appears in the English translation of the GIRM, where it had disappeared immediately after the Council. Some may wonder why the term has reappeared. Actually, it never completely went away.

838. The word "offertory" has had different meanings. Prior to the Second Vatican Council, the part of the Mass between the Creed and the preface was traditionally called the offertory. In parishes the word "offertory" has also been used colloquially to refer to the collection. _408_

839. After the Council the GIRM started distinguishing the *rites*, which it called the "preparation of the gifts" (21, 48.1, 49 [heading], 53, 80), from the *chant* sung during the rites, which it called the "offertory" (17, 21, 50, 80c, 100, 324). "Preparation of the gifts" better described what happened at this part of the Mass; the offering of the sacrifice takes place during the Eucharistic Prayer. This rite "is not in itself the sacrifice or offering but _595_ is instead a preparation for the Eucharistic Prayer, the great act of blessing and thanksgiving that constitutes the Church's memorial offering of

Christ's sacrifice, and for Holy Communion" (IOM 100). But there was a long tradition behind calling the chant an offertory.

840. The distinction between these terms was lost, however, in the first English translations of the postconciliar GIRM, which eliminated the word "offertory." The Latin word for "offertory" was retranslated as "preparation of the gifts" (17) or as "presentation [of the gifts]" (50 [twice], 80c, 100, 324) and omitted in one instance (21). This was unnecessary; in Latin the GIRM's word "offertory" referred to the song. In another place the Latin expression for "preparation of the gifts" was rendered in English as "presentation of the gifts" (21).

841. The meaning of the Latin word for "offertory" was less clear in two of these paragraphs from the pre-2002 GIRM (21 and 80c), where it could have referred to the rites. However, given the other usages of the word, these instances surely also referred to the chant. Paragraph 21 used both terms, instructing people to sit during the "preparation of the gifts" at the "offertory." The English translation of 21, probably in an attempt to sort out any confusion, removed the words "at the offertory" from that sentence. In Latin, 80c detailed the elements that can be brought by the faithful to the sanctuary at the "offertory." The English translation of 80c rendered this "at the presentation of the gifts," but the word "offertory" probably referred to the chant.

842. The 2002 GIRM retained the postconciliar Latin usages of the terms for "offertory" and "preparation of the gifts," but it wavered when it inserted the word "offertory" in one additional place. The 2002 GIRM still refers to the offertory chant (37, 74 [twice], 139, 142, 367). It still calls this part of the Mass (73–76) the "preparation of the gifts" (73 [heading]), an expression repeated in 214 to describe the same rites (139–146), and in 33, 43, 72, and 77. The cumbersome phrase in the former paragraph 21 remains unchanged in 43, now more fully translated in English as "the Preparation of the Gifts at the Offertory," where "offertory" probably refers to the chant. But the 2002 GIRM deleted one reference to the offertory antiphon (formerly 50) and replaced it with a new expression: "Singing may always accompany the rite at the offertory" (74), which contrasts the singing (otherwise called the offertory) with the offertory (here referring to the preparation of the gifts). The former 80c (now 118c), which lists the elements brought by the faithful to the altar at the "offertory," now clarifies that this is done in procession. In all cases of the 2002 GIRM, the word for "offertory" in Latin is rendered "offertory" in English, and the

Latin expression for "preparation of the gifts" is so translated in English. The neologism "presentation of the gifts" has been discarded.

STANDING FOR THE EUCHARISTIC PRAYER

843. In the United States the faithful are asked to kneel for the Eucharistic Prayer following the *Holy, Holy*, until after the doxology and Amen. This has long been the custom in the United States, even though it varies from the universal practice and early tradition of the Church. Not even RS included standing for the Eucharistic Prayer within its catalogue of contemporary abuses. Universally, standing is permitted when kneeling is prevented "by reasons of health, lack of space, the large number of people present, or some other good reason" (GIRM 43). In 2002 the American bishops further restricted this statement by prefacing it with the words "on occasion."

844. The IOM explains that people kneel in adoration (28) and "as a human gesture of submission," "penitence for sin, humility, reverence, and adoration" (31). But the GIRM says the role of the faithful during the Eucharistic Prayer is to confess the great deeds of God and offer sacrifice (2, 78), not specifically to submit, repent, or adore. An "interior disposition and outward expression of supreme reverence and adoration" acknowledges the real presence of Christ in the Eucharist at Mass, but even more so on days such as Holy Thursday and the Most Holy Body and Blood of Christ, when the faithful may "venerate this wonderful Sacrament by a special form of adoration" (GIRM 3). There are good *550* reasons to kneel in those circumstances.

845. However, the universal GIRM permits the assembly to stand for the Eucharistic Prayer for "good reason." There are many good reasons. *551*

> a. Encouraging the faithful to stand for the entire Eucharistic Prayer would enhance active participation. Unifying the posture of the entire assembly would demonstrate that the Eucharistic Prayer belongs to all the people, not just to the priest.
>
> b. Standing is the common posture for prayer throughout the Mass. Whenever the priest and the faithful address God, they stand. Having everyone stand for the Eucharistic Prayer would establish a consistent posture for prayer throughout the liturgy.
>
> c. The Eucharistic Prayer begins with the preface dialogue and ends with the doxology and Amen. The faithful assume two

different postures during this one liturgical unit. A common posture throughout the Eucharistic Prayer would clarify the unity of this text.

d.   The Fathers of the early Church invited Christians to stand for prayer to signify their faith in the resurrection. By standing for the Eucharistic Prayer, the faithful would demonstrate their belief in life after death and connect with the historical precedents of early Christians.

e.   Other churches and ecclesial communities stand for similar prayer. The faithful could harmonize their posture with the practice of other believers.

f.   All four Eucharistic Prayers contained within the OM have Latin expressions referring to the assembly as those standing at or around the altar. By actually doing so, the faithful would lend authenticity to the texts of the Mass.

846.   These reasons were set aside in the United States by the insertion of the phrase "on occasion." The resulting sentence does not completely make sense. The circumstances of ill health, lack of space, and large numbers of people are often chronic, not occasional. People of poor health who are unable to kneel on one Sunday will be unable to kneel on the occasion of the next one. The good reasons for having everyone stand throughout the Eucharistic Prayer remain, even though the legislation in the United States has asked the practice to stop with a grammatically imperfect sentence.

Sign of Peace

847.   The 2002 GIRM introduced new legislation concerning the sign of peace. The priest is not to leave the sanctuary (154), and the faithful are to offer peace only to those nearest and in a sober manner (82).

848.   In some communities the priest enters the nave to greet a number of the faithful. However, the point of this ritual is for all present to share peace, not for the priest to share peace individually with all. Where the priest had entered the nave to greet a few of the faithful, it now seems aloof for him to remain in the sanctuary. Curiously, the rubrics now allow the priest to share peace with some of the faithful at funerals and weddings, presumably family members of those for whom the event is celebrated. But this lays another meaning onto the rite of peace, mak-

ing it a time for condolence or congratulation, which is not specifically its purpose. In that context it would be more authentic to the meaning of the sign if the priest shared peace with a few of the faithful on more ordinary occasions.

639

849. In some communities the faithful have taken a long time to share peace. This rite is preparatory and subordinate to the Communion of the faithful. Balance needs to be maintained. Still, by asking the faithful to offer peace only to those nearest and in a sober manner, the 2002 GIRM imprecisely assumes that exuberance and peace are mutually *641* exclusive.

850. These new restrictions imply the Vatican's alliance with complaints about the way some people had been expressing peace. The Church should not be arguing over the sign of peace. The very purpose of this ritual is to build up peace, communion, and charity. The world needs more ways to express peace, not fewer.

COMMUNION UNDER BOTH KINDS

851. The GIRM and OM remain ambivalent about offering Communion under both kinds. They recognize the significance of this practice, but they still restrict it. A heightened sense of the real presence of Christ and fears of spilling the cup caused some authorities to judge incongruously that reverence for the Eucharist demands withholding the cup rather than offering it. In the past this opinion held sway for many centuries, when the faithful came to Mass to adore the host rather than to receive Communion. Jesus gave his Body and Blood first to be consumed, not first to be adored.

720

852. The GIRM promotes Communion under both kinds, but the Catholic Church has been unable to make the simple statement that it should be the norm at every Mass. The OM, which tells the priest to say "The Body of Christ" when giving Communion to the faithful, never mentions that a minister should say "The Blood of Christ" when giving Communion from the cup. With the guidance of universal norms, the diocesan bishop determines the precise occasions for including the faithful in Communion under both kinds (GIRM 283, 387). In practice, Communion under both kinds is more common than in the past, but by no means universal.

853. In the United States IOM 134 promotes Communion from the cup by citing Luke 22:20 (the sign of the new covenant), Matthew 26:29 (a

foretaste of the heavenly banquet), and Mark 10:38-39 (a participation in the suffering Christ). It fails to cite the most obvious text, where Jesus takes the cup at the Last Supper, hands it to the disciples and says, "Drink" (Matthew 26:27). Another missing citation comes from a discourse during Jesus' ministry: "Unless you eat the flesh of the Son of Man and drink his blood, you have no life in you" (John 6:53). Jesus never said the cup was optional. Still, although "the pastor or priest celebrant should see to its full and proper implementation," the Communion of the faithful from the cup is limited to those occasions established by the USCCB and the diocesan bishop (IOM 136). The diocesan bishop who promotes Communion under both kinds at all Masses stands close to the command of Christ.

854. An unlikely symbol surfaced in the effort to offer Communion under both kinds, namely, flagons. Flagons filled with wine had become an essential tool for parishes, which had them resting on the altar through-out the Eucharistic Prayer, in keeping with then current norms. Flagons kept the altar neat so that the bread and wine could easily be seen by the faithful, and the pouring of cups mirrored the breaking of bread during the fraction rite. The exclusion of flagons from the Communion rite has caused parishes either to cover the altar with many corporals and vessels throughout the Eucharistic Prayer or to avoid offering the cup to the faith-ful. Flagons could be put back to use and purified with other vessels.

103, 468

Extraordinary Ministers of Holy Communion

855. After the Council extraordinary ministers of Holy Communion in many parishes were invited to break bread, pour cups, receive Com-munion with the priest and deacon (in some cases after the Communion of the faithful), lift their own vessels from the altar, open the tabernacle, and cleanse the vessels. All these actions have now been restricted. In addition, the priest is asked to drink from a chalice bigger than everyone else's. And the GIRM neglected to describe the single most important ac-tion of Communion ministers: receiving Communion. To some, the new legislation stopped the blurring of clergy and laity. To others, it created clericalism at the Communion rite, when the attention of worshipers should be on their oneness in Christ.

708, 714, 716

856. The broadening of responsibilities of Communion ministers had some benefits. It expressed their cooperation and unity in faith and min-istry with deacons and priests. It kept the Mass from becoming unduly prolonged. It increased the number of those demonstrating the reverence due to sacred vessels.

648

857. The new restrictions seek to distinguish the ministry of the priest from that of the Communion ministers, but by this point in the Mass the priest's role has been clearly established. The changed practices made some of the faithful sense an unnecessary separation of clergy and laity at the very moment all are celebrating Communion. Further, these changes discounted the widespread experience of parish ministers who had crafted a Communion rite that honored the manifold gifts of the Spirit and expressed a reverence for the Eucharist by a smooth ritual action. They also made some Communion ministers feel their service was underappreciated.

858. At their worst, the new rules made it appear to some that offering Communion from the cup is more burdensome than spiritual, that too many ministers distribute Communion, and too many people come to Communion. At their best, they mean to establish uniformity in the Communion rite and to distinguish roles more carefully. The Communion rite needs to express all the values of ministry, order, reverence, and communion. It can be done effectively with broader responsibilities for extraordinary ministers of Holy Communion.

PREPARING FOR LITURGY

859. The rubrics also stress the importance of preparing for liturgy (GIRM 352, 361). Parishes can always do better at heeding this practical advice. Texts should be chosen with care, and hearts should be disposed for prayer. There should be harmony and diligence among the many ministers in the preparation and celebration of the Mass (111). Just as the celebration of the liturgy honors the many gifts of the Spirit, so too does the preparation of the liturgy. When all is done in harmony, the faithful are already experiencing communion with Christ in the Spirit.

SOME GENERAL MATTERS

ABUSES

860. The identification of certain problem areas as "liturgical abuses" (RS 48, 52, 55, 73, 79, 83, 94, 115, 126) has had both positive and negative results. It is important to approach the rubrics of the Mass with respect and care because its mystery is too great for words, too profound for actions, and too awesome for human disputation. But some words and deeds identified as abuses have come from faithful hearts searching for

ways to awaken a local community to the mysteries of the divine. They have not been malevolent, as the word "abuse" implies. When local communities experience the presence of God outside the liturgy in shared ministries, selfless service, and nature's astonishing perfection in ordinary life, they will naturally seek to import these insights into worship, so that worship and service might fit hand in hand. To recast such a spiritual desire as a liturgical abuse disregards the service of the people of God, their natural spiritual hungers, and their zeal for bringing authenticity to worship. Correction can happen with the same harmony idealized by the rubrics and the gospel if the entire Church remains open to the Spirit in preparation for, and as a result of, its worship.

861.   It disappointed many that a Roman Catholic document on abuses at the beginning of the twenty-first century dealt with the liturgy and not the sexual offenses of priests. Especially in the United States, where the words "abuse" and "Catholic Church" have been linked for too many years with sexual offense and mismanagement by leadership, it looked callous for a Roman document to explore these themes in reference to the way that priests and people pray, ignoring a far deeper problem. Victims of sexual abuse might agree that priests should vest properly for Mass and not snap the host during the consecration, but they would probably call such behavior errors, misuses, or misunderstandings. They know what abuse is, and it is not a lengthy fraction rite at the Mass.

862.   From a pastor's perspective, other liturgical matters need attention: the conscious, active, and fruitful participation of the faithful (GIRM 5); people eager to fill the front rows in churches; the skill of musicians and the singing of congregations; the quality of preaching; and the mutual appreciation of the work of bishops and the experience of parish liturgy. The proper execution of gestures and bows seems a minor matter to pastors alert to the uncertain events that plague the faithful, who wonder where God is amid loss of life, the threat of terror, a money-hungry culture, a widening gap between rich and poor, the easy procurement of abortions, the casual divorce of marriages, and the challenges of passing on the values of faith and worship to a younger generation whose hearts are increasingly lured by the voluptuous promises of sensuality and self-absorption. Those who celebrate the liturgy are aware of abuse at every level, and in the Eucharist they find their strength.

863. The Mass should not be confused with its rubrics any more than a building should not be confused with its blueprints, a sonata with its score, or a cake with its recipe. The finished product needs careful direction, but it also needs heart and soul. Sometimes the building comes out even more beautiful than it was planned, the performed sonata bears moving interpretations not marked in the music, and a cake tastes even better because the cook substituted an ingredient. Or something awful happens because the execution wavered too much from the plans. The Mass needs the rubrics in order to be the Mass, but it takes more than rubrics to pray.

864. The OM and GIRM describe a liturgy for a relatively small assembly. A parish will make adjustments. Some parts of Sunday Mass are not described; for example, the devotional practices on entering a church, the participation aids for the faithful, the use of a cantor's stand, clear responsibilities for altar servers, the presence of a table for the procession of the gifts, the directed gaze of the faithful at the showing of the consecrated elements, the bowing of heads for the final blessing, and the departure of the people. The documents are invaluable, but at times they seem unfamiliar with common needs. This may not be a deficiency. On the one hand, the documents give more attention to ministers than they do to the faithful. On the other hand, local dioceses and parishes are competent to celebrate the Eucharist with the guides already in place. They do not need more rubrics.

865. The spirit-filled execution of rubrics leads to a prayerful celebration of the Mass, but sometimes the rubrics become a source of strife. Some people become obsessed with them and find any variation an obstruction to prayer. In extreme cases they descend into an emotional abyss, where they fixate on small rubrical matters and divert their attention from more important issues in their personal lives and in the life of the community. A few people complain to their bishops and Vatican congregations about relatively minor matters in the liturgy. It is lamentable that the same energy is not always applied to feeding the hungry, caring for the sick, and visiting prisoners (Matthew 25:31-46).

866. By their nature rubrics straddle the worlds of spirituality and law. When the leaders of the Catholic Church create new rubrics, they aim to promote spirituality, but they also enter the world of compliance. If a local community has an idea for a smoother execution of the Communion rite,

for example, it has to deal with issues of obedience. It cannot advance suggestions that seem sensible to some of the faithful without causing scandal to others. Any over-legislation of rubrics brings resentment and stifles the creative spirit that can lift a liturgy from paper to prayer. Rubrics are dangerous. When there are too many, they draw attention to themselves and to the authorities who created them rather than toward the Eucharist they should serve.

867. Overall, however, the rubrics of the Mass help the faithful enter the spirit of celebration. They attune the assembly to the sacrifice of Christ and to the awe-filled thankfulness that warms their hearts. They help people pay attention to God's holy word and to approach the Communion table with reverence, respect, humility, and joy.

868. In the Liturgy of the Word, the rubrics express that God is speaking to the people now (GIRM 55). In the Liturgy of the Eucharist they express that the entire assembly of the faithful offers this sacrifice (78). They summon every faithful Christian to full, conscious, and active participation (386). This participation brings out the ecclesial nature of the celebration (19), showing how the gifts of each one contribute to the celebration of the whole. Christ is present in the assembly (27), and this brings great rejoicing.

869. This is why Christ died—to lift people from the despair of sin and to offer the promise of redemption. This is what the faithful celebrate at worship on Sundays: They remember that Christ died and rose. They believe that he will come again. They give thanks. And when they pray, God dwells among them for a brief hour that fills time with eternity. That hour is Sunday Mass.